REFERENCE

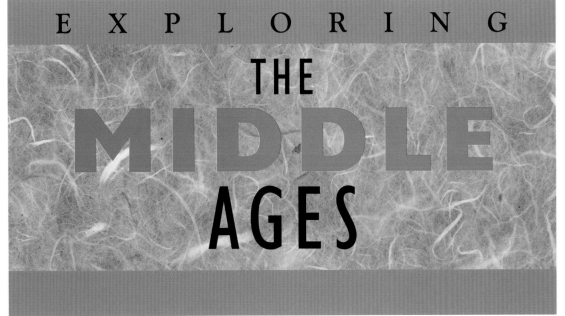

EXPLORING
THE MIDDLE AGES

2

Bayeux Tapestry – Childbirth and Midwifery

Marshall Cavendish
Reference
New York

Marshall Cavendish
99 White Plains Road
Tarrytown, New York 10591-9001

www.marshallcavendish.us

Contributing authors: Dale Anderson, Jane Bingham, Peter Chrisp, Christopher Gravett, Jen Green, Clare Hibbert, Anne Rooney, Cath Senker, Sean Sheehan, Phil Steele, Paige Weber

MARSHALL CAVENDISH
EDITOR: Thomas McCarthy
EDITORIAL DIRECTOR: Paul Bernabeo
PRODUCTION MANAGER: Michael Esposito

WHITE-THOMSON PUBLISHING
EDITORS: Alex Woolf and Steven Maddocks
DESIGN: Derek Lee and Ross George
CARTOGRAPHER: Peter Bull Design
PICTURE RESEARCH: Elaine Fuoco-Lang
INDEXER: Cynthia Crippen, AEIOU, Inc.

Library of Congress Cataloging-in-Publication Data
Exploring the Middle Ages.
    p. cm.
    Includes bibliographical references and indexes.
    Contents: 1. Abbasids-battles -- 2. Bayeux tapestry-childbirth and midwifery -- 3. Children-drama -- 4. Education-government -- 5. Greece-India -- 6. Ireland-Mamluks -- 7. Manufacturing-Nan Madol -- 8. Nobility-religion -- 9. Renaissance-sports -- 10. Surgery-women -- 11. Index.
    ISBN 0-7614-7613-X (set: lib. bdg.: alk. paper) -- ISBN 0-7614-7614-8 (v. 1: alk. paper) -- ISBN 0-7614-7615-6 (v. 2: alk. paper) -- ISBN 0-7614-7616-4 (v. 3: alk. paper) -- ISBN 0-7614-7617-2 (v. 4: alk. paper) -- ISBN 0-7614-7618-0 (v. 5: alk. paper) -- ISBN 0-7614-7619-9 (v. 6: alk. paper) -- ISBN 0-7614-7620-2 (v. 7: alk. paper) -- ISBN 0-7614-7621-0 (v. 8: alk. paper) -- ISBN 0-7614-7622-9 (v. 9: alk. paper) -- ISBN 0-7614- 7623-7 (v. 10: alk. paper) -- ISBN 0-7614-7624-5 (v. 11: alk. paper)
    1. Middle Ages--Encyclopedias. 2. Civilization, Medieval--Encyclopedias. I. Marshall Cavendish Corporation.

D114.E88 2006
909.07'03--dc22
                                  2005042161

ISBN 0-7614-7613-X (set)
ISBN 0-7614-7615-6 (vol. 2)

Printed in China

09 08 07 06 05 5 4 3 2 1

color key			
▬▬▬ Africa		▬▬▬ Oceania	
▬▬▬ Americas		▬▬▬ South and Southeast Asia	
▬▬▬ Central and East Asia		▬▬▬ Western Asia	
▬▬▬ Europe		▬▬▬ Cross-cultural articles	

Contents

Bayeux Tapestry

THE BAYEUX TAPESTRY provides a unique record of the Norman invasion of England in 1066 and the events leading up to it. Executed between 1067 and 1077, the tapestry is actually a work of embroidery, sewn in woolen thread onto unbleached linen. It contains over seventy scenes accompanied by a descriptive Latin text. Designed to be read as a narrative sequence, it was probably intended for public display in Bayeux Cathedral, in northern France.

▶ *In this scene from the Bayeux tapestry, Harold swears an oath of allegiance to William. Since the oath can be seen as justifying William's invasion of England, the inclusion of the scene suggests that the tapestry was made from a pro-Norman perspective.*

The Making of the Tapestry

The Bayeux tapestry was probably commissioned by Bishop Odo of Bayeux, half brother of William the Conqueror, with the intention of displaying it in his cathedral in Normandy. However, it was almost certainly made in southern England. In style the tapestry closely resembles Anglo-Saxon manuscripts, and it could be the product of a workshop in either Canterbury or Winchester.

Made from eight linen panels stitched together, the tapestry forms a continuous strip measuring 231 feet (70 m) in length. Its design would have first been drawn onto panels and then sewn by a team of embroiderers, using eight different colors of dyed wool. Records reveal that the tapestry was originally around twenty-five feet (8 m) longer than its present length. It probably included an extra panel depicting events after the Battle of Hastings.

Norman Propaganda?

The tapestry as it exists now shows events from 1064 to 1066. It begins with a scene

Length: 231 feet (70 m)
Depth: 20 inches (50 cm)
Human figures: 621
Horses and donkeys: 183
Dogs: 24
Ships: 37
Latin words: 2,000

showing King Edward the Confessor of England sending Harold, Earl of Wessex, to Normandy. It includes the death and burial of Edward, the coronation of Harold, and the Norman preparations for invasion. The tapestry ends with a battle sequence, including Harold's death.

It is generally agreed that the Bayeux tapestry presents the story of the conquest from a Norman perspective. The Normans claimed that William of Normandy, rather than Harold, was the true heir to the English throne. This claim is emphasized in one of the tapestry's opening scenes, where Harold is shown swearing an oath of allegiance to William, an act whose effect was to acknowledge William's superior right to the English throne.

A Valuable Record

As well as providing a record of the Norman conquest, the Bayeux tapestry contains many lively scenes of everyday life. Farmers are shown plowing fields, sowing grain, and shooting at birds with slings, while builders work with saws, hammers, and axes. There are pictures of ships, castles, churches, and cathedrals, including Westminster Abbey in London and Mont Saint Michel in northern France.

Some of the most fascinating images are found in the margins of the tapestry. Here embroiderers have depicted mythical beasts and fables, as well as small figures. Many of the marginal scenes stand completely on their own, while others relate to the main scenes.

The History of the Tapestry

The tapestry had probably reached Bayeux by 1077, when Bishop Odo consecrated the cathedral. It is certainly mentioned in an inventory of 1476, and for the next three hundred years it remained safe inside the cathedral walls. However, in 1789 it was used as a wagon cover by French revolutionaries until it was rescued by a local lawyer, and a few years later it was almost cut up to decorate a festival float. During the two World Wars the tapestry was removed to Paris for safety. It is now on public display in Bayeux.

▲ *The soldier on the right in this battle scene appears to have an arrow sticking into his face. Because the name Harold appears close to this figure, the soldier depicted being shot in the eye is thought to be King Harold.*

SEE ALSO

- **Anglo-Saxons**
- **Normans**
- **William the Conqueror**

Becket, Thomas

THOMAS BECKET (c. 1118–1170), sometimes known as Thomas à Becket, was chancellor of England from 1155 to 1162 and archbishop of Canterbury from 1162 to 1170. As chancellor Becket was the favorite of the reigning English king, Henry II. On becoming archbishop, he determined to serve the church rather than the crown. The ensuing long quarrel with Henry ended with Becket's murder in Canterbury Cathedral. Immediately revered as a martyr, Becket was canonized in 1173.

▼ *Depicted on this stained-glass window in Canterbury Cathedral is Canterbury's most famous archbishop, Thomas Becket.*

Born in Cheapside, in the heart of London, Thomas Becket was the son of a Norman merchant. In 1145 he was apprenticed to Theobald, archbishop of Canterbury, and in 1154 Theobald made Becket his archdeacon. The following year, at the recommendation of Theobald, King Henry II appointed Becket to the post of chancellor. Though known for his extravagance, Becket was loyal and hardworking. When the archbishop died in 1161, Henry made Becket Theobald's successor. Becket took his archbishopric seriously. He resigned his post as chancellor to demonstrate that his loyalty was now to the church.

Quarrel with the King

In October 1163 Henry announced plans to limit the power of ecclesiastical courts. At that time a clergyman accused of a criminal offense was tried by the church. Henry wanted "criminous clerks" tried in secular courts. He forced the bishops to accept his reforms, known as the Constitutions of Clarendon. Becket, however, continued to oppose Henry. In 1164 he was forced to flee to France, where he began a six-year exile.

In June 1170 Henry's heir, his eldest son, also called Henry and known as the Young King, was crowned by the archbishop of York. Becket was offended, since coronations were traditionally performed by the archbishop of Canterbury. Fearing that England might be placed under an interdict (an order from the pope or a bishop prohibiting the celebration of Mass and other church rites), Henry made peace with Becket at Fréteval, in France.

Becket's Murder

Back in Canterbury, Becket excommunicated the bishops involved with the coronation of the young Henry. When he heard the news, King Henry is said to have raged, "Who will rid me of this turbulent priest?" Although it is by no means certain that Henry wanted Becket dead, four knights took Henry at his word. Reginald FitzUrse, William de Tracy, Hugh de Morville, and Richard de Brito reached Canterbury on December 29, 1170, and entered the cathedral with swords drawn. When Becket refused to lift the excommunications, they murdered him.

Legacy

In 1172 the pope absolved the king, and in 1173 he canonized Becket. There were many claims of miracles at Becket's tomb. In 1174 Henry did penance at Canterbury. Millions of other pilgrims visited the shrine in the following centuries, including the fictional ones in Chaucer's *Canterbury Tales* (1390s). During the Reformation, at the order of King Henry VIII, the shrine was dismantled and Becket's bones were burned.

◄ *Four of Henry II's knights assassinated Becket on December 29, 1170, in Canterbury Cathedral. They believed, rightly or wrongly, that they were acting on the king's orders.*

IN 1158 BECKET NEGOTIATED THE BETROTHAL OF HENRY II'S HEIR TO THE DAUGHTER OF THE FRENCH KING. A CONTEMPORARY DESCRIBED BECKET'S GRAND ENTRY INTO PARIS:

He had some 200 horsemen, knights, clerks, stewards, men in waiting, men at arms and squires of noble family, all in ordered ranks. All these, and all their followers, wore bright new festal garments. He himself had 24 suits and many silk cloaks to be left behind as presents and all kinds of coloured clothes, furs, hangings and carpets. Hounds and hawks of every kind and 85 horse chariots and on every horse was a sturdy groom in a new tunic and on every chariot a warden.

WILLIAM FITZSTEPHEN, *VITA SANCTI THOMAE* (THE LIFE OF THOMAS BECKET)

SEE ALSO
- Chaucer, Geoffrey
- Monarchs
- Popes and the Papacy
- Roman Catholic Church

Bede

BEDE (C. 673–735), ALSO KNOWN AS BAEDA, was a monk, theologian, and scholar. His *Ecclesiastical History of the English People (Historia ecclesiastica gentis Anglorum)*, the first written history of England, provides a valuable record of events in Anglo-Saxon times. Bede is also famous for adopting and popularizing the method of dating events from the time of Christ's birth; this calendar eventually spread across the entire world. Within 150 years of his death, he had become known as the Venerable Bede, in recognition of both his learning and his piety.

▼ *This illustration, from a medieval manuscript, depicts Bede writing. As well as finding time for his own writing, Bede had duties as a scribe copying manuscripts for the monastery library.*

The Life of Bede

Bede was probably born at Jarrow, Northumbria. At the age of seven, he entered the nearby Monastery of Saint Peter at Wearmouth, headed by Abbot Saint Benedict Biscop. By 685 Bede had moved back to Jarrow to the Monastery of Saint Paul. An able scholar, Bede took holy orders as a deacon at age nineteen, although twenty-five was the usual age, and as a priest at age thirty.

During his lifetime Bede achieved fame for his commentaries on the Bible. He remained at Jarrow but traveled to Lindisfarne and York and may also have visited King Ceolwulf of Northumbria. When Bede died in 735, he was buried at Jarrow. His remains were later moved to Durham Cathedral.

Bede's Writings

In 703 Bede wrote *De temporibus (On Times)*, his first work on chronology, sparked by the need to reckon the date for Easter. He expanded his ideas in 725 with *De temporum ratione (On the Reckoning of Time)*.

Bede's religious writings included commentaries explaining passages from the Bible. Bede also wrote two lives of Cuthbert, Bishop of Lindisfarne (c. 721), in

This image of the four seasons comes from an eleventh-century manuscript of Bede's De Temporibus.

verse and prose, and *Historia abbatum* (*Lives of the Abbots*; c. 725). Bede's five-part *Ecclesiastical History of the English People* charted the entire course of Britain's history, from the invasion of Julius Caesar, in 55 BCE, to Bede's own time. Central to the history was England's conversion to Christianity following the arrival of Augustine of Canterbury in 597 CE.

Bede's Legacy

After his death, Bede's works were widely read, and his ideas continued to spread. One of Bede's pupils, Archbishop Egbert of York, founded the cathedral school at York, which became a center of medieval scholarship. Alcuin studied there and took Bede's ideas to the continent when he became headmaster of Charlemagne's school at Aachen, in present-day western Germany. Bede was canonized soon after his death. In 1899 he was given the title Doctor (meaning "teacher") of the Church by Pope Leo XIII.

SEE ALSO
- Anglo-Saxons
- Calendars and Clocks
- Charlemagne
- Roman Catholic Church

ONE OF BEDE'S PUPILS, CUTHWIN, DESCRIBED BEDE'S DYING DAYS IN A LETTER TO HIS FRIEND:

. . . all were sad and wept, grieving above all else at his statement that they must not expect to see his face much longer in this world. But they were heartened when he said, "If it be the will of my Maker, the time has come when I shall be freed from the body and return to Him Who created me out of nothing when I had no being. I have had a long life, and the merciful Judge has ordered it graciously. The time of my departure is at hand, and my soul longs to see Christ my King in His beauty." He also told us many other edifying things, and passed his last day happily until evening.

CITED BY LEO SHERLEY-PRICE IN HIS INTRODUCTION TO BEDE'S HISTORY OF THE ENGLISH CHURCH AND PEOPLE

Belisarius

BELISARIUS, THE LEADING BYZANTINE GENERAL of his age, was one of history's great soldiers. His victories against the Vandals of Africa and the Ostrogoths of Italy doubled the size of Byzantine territory and raised hopes, which remained unfulfilled, that the old Roman Empire might be restored. The story of Belisarius and his ungrateful treatment by Emperor Justinian has inspired dozens of poems, plays, novels, and paintings.

Early Campaigns

Belisarius (c. 505–565) was born in the Balkans, in present-day Bulgaria. As a young man he served in the imperial body-guard, commanded by the future emperor Justinian. After becoming emperor in 527, Justinian gave Belisarius command of the eastern army in a war against the Persians. In 530 Belisarius won his first victory, at Dara. Although he was beaten the following year at Callinicum, he was absolved of blame for this defeat because his soldiers had insisted on fighting against his wishes. In fact, Belisarius's defensive tactics saved his army from destruction.

Belisarius was recalled to Constantinople, where in 532 there was a widespread uprising against Justinian. Belisarius used his troops to crush this uprising; they killed around 30,000 rebels who had gathered in the Hippodrome (race track).

In 533 Belisarius led an army of just 15,000 men to North Africa, where he conquered the Vandal kingdom and captured King Gelimer. The following year Justinian allowed Belisarius to hold a triumph, an ancient Roman victory procession, the first held in Constantinople.

Belisarius then invaded the Ostrogothic kingdom of Italy and conquered Sicily (535), Naples and Rome (536), and Ravenna (540), the capital of the kingdom, where he captured King Vitigis. The

MAXIMIANVS

Ostrogoths were so impressed by his leadership and military skill that they offered to make him emperor of the West, an offer he rejected.

Late Troubles

In the 540s Belisarius fought two indecisive campaigns, against the Persians and then the Ostrogoths, who had reconquered Italy. By now he had earned the distrust of Justinian, and in 544 Belisarius was forced to retire from public life. In 559, however, when the Kutrigur Huns swept over the Danube River and threatened to take Constantinople, Justinian called on Belisarius's services again. At the head of an army of just three hundred professional soldiers supported by a large number of peasants, Belisarius made a surprise attack on the Huns. Fooled into thinking that they faced a large Byzantine army, the Huns fled back across the Danube, and Constantinople was saved.

Justinian showed no gratitude for this victory. In 562 Belisarius was accused of plotting against the emperor. His fortune was confiscated, and he was placed under house arrest. Yet there was no evidence against Belisarius, and in 563 he was released and restored to favor. His death in March 565 was followed just eight months later by that of the emperor.

◀ *Emperor Justinian, with a crown and halo, appears with his court on this mosaic from the Church of Saint Vitale in Ravenna. The man with a dark beard on Justinian's immediate right is thought to be Belisarius.*

SEE ALSO
- Balkans • Byzantine Empire
- Constantinople • Goths
- Huns • Justinian, Code of • Vandals

Benedict

SAINT BENEDICT (c. 480–547) was the founder of the Benedictine religious order. He established a great monastery at Monte Cassino in Italy and wrote a set of guidelines for his monks, which became known as the Rule of Saint Benedict. Forty years after his death, Pope Gregory the Great wrote about Benedict's life, and his fame spread rapidly. Over the next three hundred years most of the monasteries in western Europe adopted Benedict's Rule.

Early Life

Benedict was born in the small town of Nursia, in central Italy, four years after the collapse of the Roman Empire. The son of a nobleman, he was educated in Rome, but while he was still a teenager, rejecting the worldly life of the city, he abandoned his studies and went to live in the country. For a while Benedict lived with a group of men and shared their simple, hardworking way of life, but then he became a hermit and spent the next three years alone in a cave above the Subiaco valley.

The First Benedictines

Gradually, Benedict's fame spread, and many men came to see him, asking for advice on how to live their life. Benedict built twelve small monastic houses for his followers and encouraged them to live a simple life: working hard in the fields, preaching and teaching in the local community, reading and studying, and sharing regular prayers. After a few years, however, the Subiaco community began to suffer from persecution, so Benedict left to set up a new monastery.

Monte Cassino

In the high mountain village of Monte Cassino, Benedict built a single large monastery where his monks continued the pattern of life established at Subiaco. The monks cared for the poor and the sick, but they also welcomed nobles and bishops to their monastery. Benedict's fame and influence soon spread, and additional Benedictine monasteries were founded in many different parts of Italy.

▼ *This fresco from Siena, Italy, depicts Saint Benedict and his monks sharing a simple meal.*

Benedict spent the rest of his life at Monte Cassino. According to his first biographer, Pope Gregory the Great, Benedict performed many miracles there. Gregory relates that a short while before he died, Benedict was granted a glorious vision: he saw the whole world gathered together under God's divine light as if under a beam of brilliant sunlight.

The Rule of Saint Benedict

Benedict's Rule, probably written while he was at Monte Cassino, outlines his principles for the monastic life. It emphasizes the importance of manual work, study, and private prayer, reminds the monks of their duty to care for the sick and the poor, and stresses the importance of a simple way of life, with regular prayers at set hours.

> *Listen carefully, my son, to the Master's instructions, and attend to them with the ear of your heart. This is advice from a father who loves you; welcome it, and faithfully put it into practice. The labor of obedience will bring you back to him from whom you had drifted through the sloth of disobedience.*
>
> THE RULE OF SAINT BENEDICT, VV. 1–3

Legacy

Although monasteries existed long before Saint Benedict's time, monks did not follow any set rules, and some of the monastic houses were very corrupt. Benedict's Rule provided a clear framework for monks to live by. Its emphasis on study encouraged a revival of learning; indeed, the Benedictines became famous for the quality and beauty of their manuscript work.

SEE ALSO
- Christendom
- Monasticism
- Roman Catholic Church

◀ *The eleventh-century abbey at Saint Benoît-sur-Loire, in France, one of the many influential Benedictine abbeys built throughout Europe.*

Beowulf

PRESERVED IN A MANUSCRIPT dated to around the year 1000, *Beowulf* is the longest and most famous Anglo-Saxon poem. It was probably composed around 725 by a Christian poet in the court of Mercia or Northumberland. The poem itself is set in pagan times, around the early 500s. It originally had no title but was later named after its Scandinavian hero, Beowulf. There is no evidence that Beowulf ever existed, but some of the people, places, and events of the poem are part of the historical record.

▼ *The opening page of the sole surviving manuscript that contains the poem* Beowulf, *known as* Cotton Vitellius A. xv.

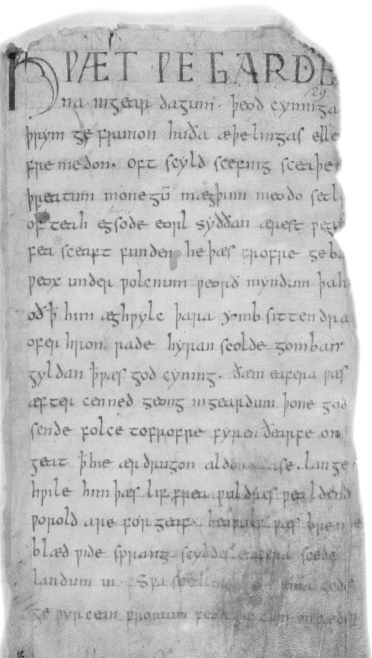

The Story

In the first part of the poem, King Hrothgar of Denmark is being menaced by an evil monster, Grendel. Beowulf, prince of the Geats of southern Sweden, visits Hrothgar's great hall, Heorot, and promises to end the terror. He bravely kills Grendel and later seeks out and kills Grendel's mother, who has come seeking revenge for her son's death. Hrothgar hosts a great feast at Heorot in Beowulf's honor.

The second part of the poem is set much later, when Beowulf has been king of the Geats for fifty years. Now a dragon is ravaging his land because someone has stolen from its hoard of treasure. Despite his age, Beowulf heroically sets out with his thanes to slay the dragon. All but one of the men desert Beowulf. There is a long battle, and Beowulf dies killing the dragon. The poem ends with Beowulf's funeral.

The Importance of *Beowulf*

Beowulf, the longest-surviving Anglo-Saxon poem, provides a useful record of Anglo-Saxon society. Life centers around the great hall, where the king or lord provides his thanes with food, drink, clothing, and armor. In return the thanes owe him loyalty in battle. The abandonment of Beowulf by the thanes during his last battle is indicative of the falling away of the old

As everyone celebrates the death of Grendel and his mother, King Hrothgar warns Beowulf against pride—death will come to him one day, too:

Beloved Beowulf, best of warriors, resist this deadly taint, take what is better, your lasting profit. Put away arrogance, noble fighter! The noon of your strength shall last for a while now, but in a little time sickness or a sword will strip it from you: either enfolding flame or a flood's billow or a knife-stab or the stoop of a spear or the ugliness of age; or your eyes' brightness lessens and grows dim. Death shall soon have beaten you then, O brave warrior!

BEOWULF

Christian times, and in the end, the story demonstrates that seeking vengeance for loss of kin is not heroic; in fact, revenge is the motive that drives Grendel's mother. The poet may also be suggesting that a quest for glory, such as Beowulf's, will inevitably end in self-destruction.

SEE ALSO
- **Anglo-Saxons**
- **Poetry**

pagan values, which are ready to be replaced by Christianity.

Beginning with J. R. R. Tolkien, the famed English author and Anglo-Saxon expert, some scholars have seen *Beowulf* as a Christian allegory, in which the hero stands for goodness and fights the evils that threaten society. Nonetheless, the ideals that Beowulf describes—including bravery, vengeance, and loyalty—belong to a pre-Christian Anglo-Saxon society, as does Beowulf's belief that a man's destiny is controlled by fate. However, the anonymous poet lived in

▶ *If he ever did exist, Beowulf would have owned a helmet similar to this one, which was discovered at a pagan ship-burial site at Sutton Hoo, in Suffolk, England, and dates to around 635.*

Berber Dynasties

THE BERBER PEOPLE were the original inhabitants of western North Africa. Their ancient language was also called Berber. They lived as farmers in well-defended mountain villages or as camel traders carrying salt and gold across the Sahara Desert. Berber society was divided into many tribes, each with its own chief. Sometimes the tribes cooperated; sometimes they warred with each other.

New Faith, New Empire

Between 700 and 900 CE many Berber tribes converted to a new faith, Islam, after Muslim Arab soldiers invaded from the Middle East. As a result of this Muslim conquest, Berber lands became part of a large, powerful empire ruled by the Abbasid dynasty in Baghdad. Some Berber tribes were friendly to their new rulers. They joined the Abbasid armies and attacked lands belonging to non-Muslims in North Africa and Spain. However, other Berbers fought against their conquerors and supported a rival Muslim dynasty, the Fatimids, who won control of North Africa from the Abbasids in 909.

The Almoravids' Fight for Power

By around 1050 Fatimid power was weakening, and Abd Allah ibn Yasin (died c. 1059), a Berber religious leader from Mauritania, began recruiting a large army of tribesmen to challenge the dynasty's power. Yasin followed a strict version of Islam and planned to force people to follow rigorous Muslim laws. His followers, who became known as Almoravids (from the Arabic al-Murabitun, meaning "people of the fortress"), made plans to invade Morocco. The next Almoravid leader, Yusuf ibn Tashufin (1061–1106), took control of all Morocco and founded a new capital, Marrakech, in 1062. He also conquered lands to the north, in Spain, and to the south, in Senegal.

Fresh Calls for Reform

The Almoravids' use of force and their severe religious laws made them unpopular. Almoravid army commanders also quarreled among themselves. Around 1120 a

▶ This Berber, pictured in the late eighteenth century by a European artist, is wearing clothes designed for desert conditions. His loose woolen robes keep him cool, and his long scarf, wound around his head, can be pulled down to protect his face from sun glare and sandstorms.

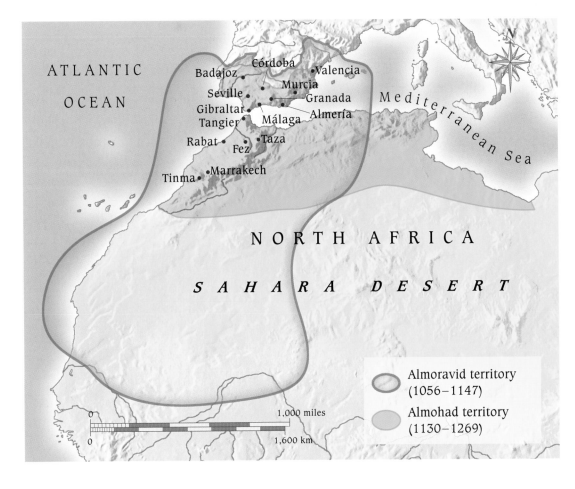

◄ *From 1056 to 1269, the Berber Almohad and Almoravid dynasties ruled a large part of northwestern Africa, together with land in southern Spain.*

Almoravid territory (1056–1147)

Almohad territory (1130–1269)

AN ALMOHAD RELIGIOUS LEADER'S ADVICE TO HIS PEOPLE:

If you see anything wrong, take action against it. If you can't take action, then speak out against it. If you can't speak out, then fight against it in your heart. This is your religious duty.

IBN TUMART

new alliance of Berber tribes from the High Atlas Mountains began to rebel against the Almoravids. They were led by Muhammad ibn Tumart (c. 1080–1130), a scholar who called for social and religious reform. He said Muslims must lead pure lives, following Islam's holy book, the Koran, and he called for a holy war against sinners. Ibn Tumart led attacks on shops selling wine and on women who did not wear veils, even though the wearing of veils went against ancient Berber tradition. Ibn Tumart's followers became known as Almohads (from the Arabic al-Muwahhidun, meaning "believers in one God").

Almohad Conquests

By 1147 Almohad soldiers had conquered most of North Africa from Morocco to Libya. By 1195 the Almohad dynasty also ruled southern Spain. Almohad leaders such as Abd al-Mumin (1133–1163) and Yakub I (1184–1199) were fierce and intolerant. Eager to encourage their own interpretation of Islam, they tried to expel all Jews and Christians from their lands.

CHRONOLOGY

1039
Ibn Yasin begins recruiting Berber tribesmen; his followers become known as Almoravids.

1062
Having conquered Morocco, Ibn Tashufin founds Marrakech.

1085–1110
Almoravids take control of southern Spain.

1120–1130
Ibn Tumart, preaching moral reform, recruits followers, the Almohads.

1133
Abd al-Mumin becomes the new Almohad leader.

1133–1147
Almohads conquer Morocco.

1147–1170
Almohads conquer Libya, Tunisia, and southern Spain.

1212
Christians regain most of Spain.

1236–1452
Hafsid dynasty conquers Tunisia and Libya.

1269–1400
Marinid dynasty conquers Morocco.

Almoravid styles in art were plain and simple, reflecting Ibn Yasin's rigid religious views. Almoravids built tall, proud towers and mosques with austere geometric decoration, and they defended their cities with massive walls and gates. Later their designs were influenced by more graceful, flowing patterns copied from southern Spain.

Almohad religious art was also based on pure geometric patterns, especially in carved wood and plaster. These patterns were often combined with twisting, curving motifs that imitated the shape of leaves and flowers. Almohad rulers also built luxurious palaces with fountains, gardens, and libraries.

The Bab Aganou gate at Marrakech, Morocco, built by the Almohad ruler Yakub I in the late twelfth century. Richly decorated with geometric patterns, the gate's horseshoe-shaped arch is similar to Muslim structures in southern Spain.

Almohad rulers, great patrons of art and learning, encouraged Muslim teachers with moderate views and invited some of the greatest Muslim scholars, including the scientist, doctor, and philosopher Ibn Rushd (1126–1198), known in Europe as Averroes, to live at their courts.

Defeat and Decay

The Almohads relied on loyal relatives from their own Berber tribe to rule their vast empire but nevertheless found it difficult to stay in power. In 1212 they lost most of their land in Spain after Christian kings defeated them at Las Navas de Tolosa. In 1229 their Berber rivals, the Hafsid dynasty, took control of Tunisia. Almohad power finally collapsed when another Berber dynasty, the Marinids, captured Marrakech in 1269.

Two Lesser Dynasties

The Marinids built a new capital at Fez and then spent many years fighting in Africa and Spain. However, warring weakened and impoverished them, and they slowly lost control of Morocco. They were finally overthrown in 1465 by the Wattasid dynasty.

The Hafsid dynasty traded with Italy, Spain, and southern France and maintained a pirate fleet to plunder Mediterranean shipping. Even so, it could never match Almohad power. In 1452 the Hafsid dynasty collapsed because of family power struggles, and its territories fell to the Turkish Ottoman Empire in 1574.

SEE ALSO

- Abbasids • Arabs • Fatimids
- Islam • Ottomans • Spanish Kingdoms

Black Death

IN THE MID-FOURTEENTH century a disastrous outbreak of plague devastated the known world. Later known as the Black Death, the plague began in central Asia and reached southern Italy in 1347. For the next six years the Black Death raged through Europe and killed up to one-third of the population. As people were unaware that the plague was carried by blood-sucking fleas that lived on rats, they were powerless to prevent its spread.

The Black Death was probably an outbreak of bubonic plague, a highly infectious disease that had occurred before the Middle Ages and was to return to Europe many times after the 1340s. Bubonic plague broke out in central Asia in 1346 and spread rapidly through India and the Middle East.

In October 1347 the Black Death reached southern Europe when a ship full of infected soldiers returned from Asia to the island of Sicily, just off the coast of Italy. Within three months the plague spread to mainland Italy, and a couple of months later it traveled as far north as France. By the summer of 1348, central Germany was infected, and before the end of the year, the plague reached southern Britain.

During 1349 the Black Death raced through northern Europe and reached Sweden by 1350. By 1351 most of Europe was free of infection, but the disease continued to rage in northern Russia until 1353. In the continent of Europe, only a few places, the largest being a remote area of present-day Poland, remained entirely untouched by plague.

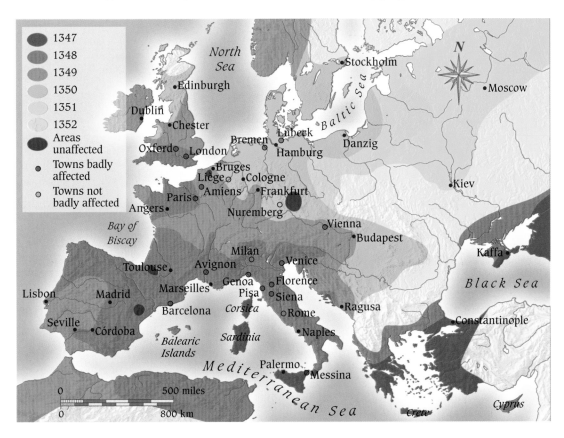

Legend:
- 1347
- 1348
- 1349
- 1350
- 1351
- 1352
- Areas unaffected
- Towns badly affected
- Towns not badly affected

This map shows the spread of the Black Death through Europe between the years 1347 and 1353.

E nfuere alerent chascu lor
M eslier lor eneit r besoing
M out lor content agete loing.
L i filz le roi furent ploze
L nor qui furent enterre

S arqeus oren
S iles muttret e
D elez leur fre
E nteere furer

Apens fuerit r enseter

N la plus belle
S ouz cel na c
N ela plus bell

This fourteenth-century manuscript page depicts victims of the plague being carried out of a house to be burned or buried.

Symptoms and Treatment

The Black Death was probably given its name because of the black boils, or buboes, that were one of its early symptoms. Buboes, filled with blood and pus, first appeared in the armpits and groin of victims and were often followed by black or red blotches that spread rapidly over the body. Other symptoms included a high fever, spitting of blood, and pneumonia. Most victims died within a few days of developing the disease, and some died within merely a few hours.

Most medieval doctors thought the Black Death was caused by "infection of the air" and attempted to purge the atmosphere by burning sulfur or boiling herbs. Many, however, also realized that the plague was spread by contact with victims and even with their clothing, and in some places victims' clothes were burned after their death as a public health measure. Unfortunately, these and similar well-intentioned measures could do very little to stop the spread of a disease that was actually carried by rats and fleas.

As well as being powerless to stop the spread of the Black Death, medieval doctors also could do nothing to treat its symptoms. Many doctors practiced blood-letting, and contemporary accounts describe the range of potions created by doctors and chemists, some of which contained mercury and gold.

Reactions

The Black Death caused widespread panic and despair. Many people believed the plague was a punishment from God for their sinful behavior and sought his forgiveness. One extreme form of penitential practice involved the formation of groups of self-flagellants—men and women who, walking through the cities of Europe, lashed themselves with a whip in a public demonstration of guilt and sorrow.

While many blamed their own sinfulness for the disaster of the plague, some looked around for others to blame. In large parts of Spain, the Arabs were suspected of spreading the Black Death; pilgrims and lepers were also blamed for spreading corruption. Jews, too, were often targeted as the guilty party. In cities throughout Europe, Jews in the thousands, unjustly accused of poisoning the water supplies, were put to death.

Reactions to the Black Death in Florence are vividly documented by the Italian writer Giovanni Boccaccio, who lived through the catastrophe. In the prologue to *The Decameron*, his great collection of tales, Boccaccio describes how a mass of people fled from the city in panic. Some resorted to a totally self-indulgent lifestyle, and some even looted the homes of the sick and the dead. While a few individuals cared for the sick and dying, many others were so overwhelmed by panic that they abandoned even their closest relatives.

▼ *As the Black Death raged through Europe, bands of hooded flagellants punished themselves in the hope of gaining forgiveness from God. Sometimes they left their back exposed so that they could whip themselves more easily.*

GIOVANNI BOCCACCIO DESCRIBED THE RESPONSE OF THE PEOPLE OF FLORENCE TO THE BLACK DEATH:

. . . this sore affliction entered so deep into the minds of men and women that, in the horror thereof, brother was forsaken by brother, nephew by uncle . . . and often husband by wife; nay, what is more and scarcely to be believed, fathers and mothers were found to abandon their own children, untended, unvisited, to their fate, as if they had been strangers.

THE DECAMERON

CATAPULTING CORPSES

The fifteenth-century Italian chronicler Gabriel de Mussis left a dramatic account of how Europeans were first infected by the Black Death. He records that in 1346 an army of Tartars besieged the city of Kaffa (in present-day Ukraine), which was a base for Italian merchants. In order to bring the siege to a rapid end, the Tartar army catapulted the corpses of plague victims over the city walls. According to de Mussis, the Italians soon caught the infection and carried the plague back with them to Sicily. There are, however, some problems with this colorful account. De Mussis was not an eyewitness but heard the story from returning sailors. Also, bubonic plague was spread not by contact with corpses but by contact with fleas that lived on rats.

▼ *Bubonic plague was very hard to stamp out, and outbreaks continued throughout the centuries. This woodcut shows the weekly burial of victims in London in 1665.*

Consequences

The most obvious effect of the Black Death was depopulation, as over 75 million people were wiped out in six years. Landlords lost large numbers of farmworkers, and many merchants and traders were ruined. This economic upheaval led to rapid inflation and widespread poverty, as food prices rose dramatically. Towns were worst affected, as rural people could resort to subsistence farming for food.

One consequence of the drastically reduced population was that farm labor was in great demand. Many farmworkers used their bargaining power to change their status from vassal to freeman (vassals were tied to a particular lord, while freemen were free to work for whomever they wished). As freemen, laborers could travel to find better-paid work, and this increased mobility of labor played an important part in the decline of feudalism in the fifteenth and sixteenth centuries.

Following the sufferings of the Black Death and the resulting economic decline, there was a widespread sense of discontent. All over Europe people became more critical of their landlords, whom they blamed for exploitation, and this sense of resentment contributed to the wave of peasant uprisings in Europe during the fourteenth and fifteenth centuries.

SEE ALSO

- Boccaccio, Giovanni
- Death and Burial
- Disease
- Feudalism
- Medicine and Healing
- Plague

Boccaccio, Giovanni

THE ITALIAN POET AND SCHOLAR Giovanni Boccaccio (1313–1375) is best known for his collection of one hundred tales, *The Decameron*. He was a pioneer of vernacular literature and the first to use ottava rima, a form that came to typify Italian verse. He emphasized that a man could overcome fortune rather than be its victim and played down the role of divine intervention in human affairs. For this attitude, which came to be called humanism, he is often considered one of the founders of the Renaissance.

Early Years

The son of a merchant banker, Boccaccio was probably born in Florence. In 1327 he moved to Naples to study business and law but after a few years turned to literature instead. He read works by a fellow Italian, Petrarch, and mixed with courtly society. Boccaccio wrote two romances in Naples, *Il filocolo* and *Il filostrato*—the latter the story of Troilus and Cressida. In 1341 he returned to Florence and completed *The Teseida,* an epic in ottava rima about two friends in love with the same woman.

The Writer Matures

Boccaccio composed his major work, *The Decameron,* between 1348 and 1353. It is a collection of stories narrated by ten young noblemen and women who have fled plague-ridden Florence. During their stay in a country palazzo, each tells a story a day. The resulting tales are comic, often bawdy, and masterfully written, with characters covering the spectrum of medieval society. Corruption in the church is a recurring theme, but the emphasis is on the sheer joy of being human.

Last Years

While writing *The Decameron*, Boccaccio began his career as a Florentine ambassador. He also became friends with Petrarch, a champion of vernacular literature. However, Boccaccio wrote nothing of note in Italian after *The Decameron*. His most important later work, a biography of Dante, was in Latin.

Seventy-five years after his death, Boccaccio was honored as a famous Florentine in a wall painting by Andrea del Castagno. Two other poets appear on the fresco: Dante and Petrarch.

▲ *A depiction by Botticelli of a tale from* The Decameron. *A nobleman, Nastagio degli Onesti, sees a recurring phantom scene: a girl is killed by a knight and torn apart by his hounds. Both have been condemned to hell—he for suicide, she for driving him to it. When Nastagio's own cruel beloved sees the scene, she agrees to marry him.*

It is possible that Boccaccio came to regret the immoral tales of *The Decameron*, because in 1362 Petrarch wrote to him urging him not to burn his writings. Fortunately for posterity he never did. In 1363 poverty forced Boccaccio to leave Florence; he returned briefly, ten years later, but soon left in ill health and died in the village of Certaldo.

Legacy

Boccaccio was enormously influential in medieval times, and his work is still read. *Il filostrato* was the source for the English poet Geoffrey Chaucer's *Troilus and Criseyde*. In the *Canterbury Tales*, Chaucer also employs a group of characterful narrators, a device inspired by *The Decameron*.

SEE ALSO
- **Black Death** • **Chaucer, Geoffrey**
- **Dante** • **Florence** • **Literature**
- **Petrarch** • **Poetry**

Bohemia

THE MEDIEVAL KINGDOM OF BOHEMIA, located in the present-day Czech Republic, had its capital at Prague, on the Vltava River. Czechs formed the greater part of the population, but Germans and Jews were also numbered among the inhabitants. In the tenth century Bohemia became part of the Holy Roman Empire and reached the height of its power in the thirteenth and fourteenth centuries. In the 1400s it was torn apart by religious wars.

The name Bohemia derives from the Boii, a Celtic tribe that was displaced by Germanic invaders about two thousand years ago. The Bohemian territory lay beyond the borders of the Roman Empire. By 500 CE it had been invaded from the east by Slavic peoples, including the Czechs. For a time the region came under the rule of another group of invaders, the Avars, but they were defeated by Samo, a Czech leader who died in 658.

Premysl and His Successors

Later rulers traced their dynastic origins to aň eighth-century Czech princess called Libuse, who was said to have married a peasant called Premysl. The Czechs beca̅me part of a kingdom called Great Moravia and conve̅rted to Christianity in about 873. After Moravia was broken up by attacking Magyars (Hungarians), a new Bohemian kingdom emerged. Its ruler, Wenceslaus the Good, who was murdered by his brother Boleslaw in 929, was later elevated to sainthood. In 950 Boleslaw was forced to recognize Otto I, the Holy Roman emperor, as his overlord.

Bohemia's Golden Age

In the twelfth and thirteenth centuries Bohemia achieved a powerful position within the Holy Roman Empire and acquired new territory. Many Germans settled in the kingdom. Bohemia's expansion ended in 1278, when Rudolf I, the recently elected king of Germany and the founder of the powerful Hapsburg dynasty, gained Austria and Styria.

▼ *This Bohemian painting depicting the cycle of the months, dating from about 1400, shows January in a snowball fight with courtiers. Stenico Castle, pictured here, lies within the mountainous region of Trentino, in northern Italy.*

▶ *A monument to the religious reformer Jan Hus stands in Prague as an enduring symbol of Bohemia's independent spirit.*

JAN HUS c. 1369–1415

Jan Hus was born at Husinec in Bohemia. He studied theology at the University of Prague and lectured there from 1398. He was inspired by John Wycliffe, an English religious reformer who died in 1384. Hus condemned the church as ridden with superstition, greed, and corruption. He was excommunicated in 1411, and in 1415, having been tried and convicted by the Council of Constance, he was burned at the stake as a heretic. His followers, known as Hussites, took up arms, and war raged in Bohemia until 1434. His teachings survive to the present day in a Christian denomination known as the Unity of the Brethren.

The Přemyslid dynasty came to an end in 1306, and John of Luxembourg was chosen as king of Bohemia in 1310. His son Charles IV was crowned Holy Roman Emperor in 1355. Prague became a center of the arts and scholarship, its university dating from 1348. The preeminence of the Czech language encouraged a sense of independence among Bohemian Slavs.

Religious Strife

In the early fifteenth century this independent spirit manifested itself in rebellion against religious orthodoxy. Civil war erupted in Bohemia between supporters of the reformer Jan Hus and armies loyal to the pope. By 1436 peace was restored in Bohemia (conflict resumed in the next century with the Protestant Reformation). In 1526 Bohemia came under Hapsburg rule, but the powder keg of religion and nationalism blew up once again in 1618, when the Thirty Years War began.

SEE ALSO
• Hapsburgs • Holy Roman Empire

CHRONOLOGY

873
The Czechs adopt the Christian faith.

950
Bohemia becomes part of the Holy Roman Empire.

1198
Ottakar I is crowned king; Bohemia becomes wealthy.

1350
Under Emperor Charles IV, a golden age of Bohemian culture begins.

1415
The burning of Jan Hus starts the Hussite Wars.

Bruges

BRUGES, LOCATED IN FLANDERS, in present-day Belgium, was one of the wealthiest towns in medieval Europe and a center of the cloth trade. The rapid growth of its merchant class from the twelfth century was an indication of the increasing importance of commerce and banking in western Europe in the later Middle Ages. These activities began to transform an economy based on land ownership and services, which had earlier been dominant.

Both Gauls and Romans traded along the coasts of Flanders. When the Roman Empire fell in 476, the region was overrun by the Franks. The greatest of the Frankish rulers, Charlemagne (747–814), incorporated Flanders into his empire. When Charlemagne died, the empire was divided, and Flanders became part of the French kingdom.

However, from 862 the counts of Flanders, acting with increasing independence, started a long power struggle. Baldwin II built a stronghold called Bruges (in the Flemish language, Brugge) at a crossing of the Reie River and fortified it against attack from the Vikings. From 957 a seasonal fair was established there to market textiles.

▼ *This map of 1572 shows the heart of the medieval city of Bruges, in Flanders.*

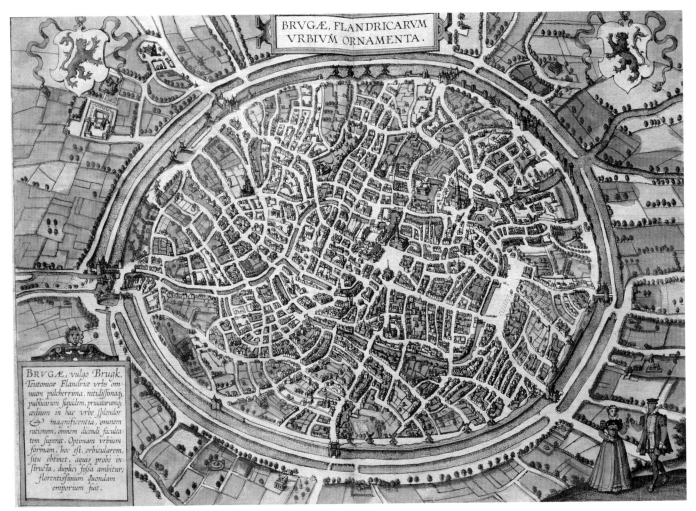

BRVGÆ, FLANDRICARVM VRBIVM ORNAMENTA.

BRVGÆ, vulgo Brugk, Teutonicæ Flandriæ vrbs omnium pulcherrima, nitidissimaq, publicarum siquidem, priuatarumq, ædium in hac vrbe splendor & magnificentia, omnem rationem, omnem dicendi facultatem superat. Optimam vrbium formam, hoc est, orbicularem, situ obtinet, aquis probe instructa, duplici fossa ambitur; florentissimum quondam emporium fuit.

CITY OF PAINTERS

Bruges was a center not just of crafts but of fine art funded by wealthy patrons. The city's greatest painter was Jan van Eyck, who moved to Bruges probably in 1430 and died there in 1441. Van Eyck mastered painting with oils and excelled in the representation of light and of realistic detail. The German-born artist Hans Memling, an inspired painter of religious subjects and portraits, also lived in Bruges, from 1461 until 1494.

A Merchant City

When floods swept in from the North Sea in 1134, a new estuary of the Zwijn River was formed. This estuary brought the coastline nearer to the city, which now had its port at Damme. Bruges prospered through trade with North Sea, Baltic, and Mediterranean ports.

Foreign merchants and bankers, many of them Italians and Lombards, made their homes here. Enjoying considerable autonomy, Bruges became not just the capital of Flanders but one of Europe's leading mercantile cities.

A new port called Sluis was built for Bruges in 1290, and in 1297 Bruges itself was greatly expanded. In 1300 it became a crucial link in the northern European trading network known as the Hanseatic League. The city had great warehouses and a splendid town hall, built in 1370. The wealthy van der Beurs family gave its name to the *beurs* (that is, the bourse, or stock exchange). The merchants who traded in cloth, known as *poorters*, formed a social elite that enjoyed many privileges. The aristocracy began to envy the power and wealth of these merchants, as did poorer craft workers and laborers.

Conflict and Decline

Battles with the French were common. In 1302 the people of Bruges rose up against French troops occupying their city. Flanders also became a battleground between England and France in the Hundred Years War (1337–1453). Indeed, a naval battle in 1340, off Sluis, the port of Bruges, was the most important engagement in the opening years of that war. The French lost 200 ships to the English and suffered about 30,000 casualties in hand-to-hand fighting.

In 1369 Margaret, heiress to the County of Flanders, married Philip the Bold, duke of Burgundy. The Burgundians were deeply involved in the Anglo-French wars of this period and needed to raise taxes to pay their armies. Their fiscal demands caused anger and resentment in Bruges.

In 1482 rule passed to the Hapsburg dynasty. By then the fortunes of Bruges had taken a turn for the worse, for the Zwijn River was rapidly becoming blocked by sediment. Trade moved to rival cities, such as Ghent and Antwerp.

CHRONOLOGY

957
Bruges becomes a trading center for woolen cloth.

1134
Changing coastline brings Bruges nearer to the sea.

1297
Bruges is greatly expanded, with new city walls.

1369
The duke of Burgundy becomes count of Flanders and thus ruler of Bruges.

1482
After rule passes to the Hapsburgs, Bruges declines.

SEE ALSO
- Burgundy • Charlemagne
- Cities and Towns • Flanders • France
- Hapsburgs • Hanseatic League
- Hundred Years War

Buddhism

BUDDHISM IS A TRADITION OF THOUGHT and religious practice founded in northern India by a prince called Siddhartha Gautama (c. 563–483 BCE). The teachings of Siddhartha, known as the Buddha, or "enlightened one," spread rapidly through eastern Asia in the early Middle Ages. Adherents of Buddhism seek spiritual enlightenment above all else. Humans must improve themselves over many lives on earth before attaining nirvana, a state that unites the individual with the infinite.

Lands of the Buddha

By the year 500 CE Buddhism was established in India and Sri Lanka, across central Asia, in Korea, and in China, and it was beginning to spread across Southeast Asia. Buddhism reached Japan in 538 and Tibet during the 600s.

Buddhism was spread by monks who traveled far and wide, teaching people about the life of the Buddha. In 630 the Chinese monk Hsüan-tsang began a fifteen-year journey to India to bring Buddhist scriptures back to the city of Chang'an. Merchants also spread the faith as they sailed the Indian Ocean or traveled to China along the central Asian trading routes known collectively as the Silk Road.

Some countries, such as Japan, made Buddhism the official state religion. In 1056 a Burman king, Anawratha, converted to Buddhism and started a period of intensive temple building in Burma (present-day Myanmar). The remains of 2,217 temples still surround his capital, Bagan.

Elsewhere, however, the tide of Buddhism was already beginning to turn. Other beliefs and religions, such as traditional Hinduism and Confucianism, recovered ground. Muslim armies were invading northern India. By 1500 Buddhism's strongholds were in Sri Lanka, Southeast Asia, and the Tibetan plateau, while it remained influential, in combination with other religions, in China, Korea, and Japan.

▼ *The temples of Bagan, in Myanmar, many of them built in the twelfth and thirteenth centuries, are a magnificent example of Buddhism's eastward expansion.*

▶ *This map shows the eastward spread of the Buddhist faith and its principal divisions in the medieval period.*

MONGOLIA

JAPAN

CHINA

TIBET

NEPAL

INDIA

TAIWAN

PACIFIC

OCEAN

BURMA

ANNAM

THAILAND

CHAMPA

CAMBODIA

BORNEO

- ● Theravada Buddhism
- ● Mahayana Buddhism (Tibetan)
- ● Mahayana Buddhism (Chinese-Japanese)

0   1,000 miles
0   1,600 km

Buddhist Traditions

Differences that developed among the early followers of Buddhism continued to be debated during the Middle Ages. Separate traditions still exist.

One early tradition, called Theravada (the doctrine of the elders) or Hinayana (small vehicle) Buddhism, emphasized the importance of meditation, monastic life, and an individual's progess toward nirvana. Theravada dominated Sri Lanka, Myanmar, Thailand, Laos, and Cambodia. The other tradition, called Mahayana (large vehicle) Buddhism, saw enlightenment as a means of helping others and placed importance upon Buddhist sutras (scriptures). Mahayana Buddhism spread to Nepal, Tibet, China, Korea, Japan, and Vietnam.

New Beliefs

In its original form, Buddhism addressed humanity directly. Although rooted in Hindusim, it did not concern itself with the worship of gods. However, as Buddhism spread, it interacted with other spiritual traditions and adopted elements of religious worship.

Tibetan Buddhism accepted belief in spirits and magic. Chinese Buddhism

CHRONOLOGY

500–750
Mahayana Buddhist cave art is produced in the Deccan region of India.

520
Chan Buddhism arrives in China.

538
Buddhism reaches Japan.

618
With the start of the Tang dynasty, a golden age of Chinese Buddhism begins.

651
First Buddhist temple is built in Tibet.

868
World's oldest surviving printed book, the *Diamond Sutra,* is written.

935
Goreyo dynasty promotes Buddhism in Korea.

1056
First temples are built at Bagan, Myanmar.

1100s
Zen Buddhism becomes established in Japan.

1238
Temples are built in Thai kingdom of Sukhothai.

THE WAY OF ZEN

In about 520 CE an Indian monk, Bodhidharma, brought a new form of meditation to China. It became known as Chan in Chinese, Son in Korean, and Zen in Japanese. It was brought to Japan by the monk Eisai, who lived from 1141 to 1215. Zen emphasizes the importance of meditation under strict rules. It rejects both religious rites and intellectual thought. Instead, it poses koans (riddles) that challenge reason. One example is "When you clap both hands together you hear a sound. Now listen to the sound of one hand clapping." The aim is to achieve satori (enlightenment), which some schools of Zen argue can happen in a sudden flash of recognition.

▼ *This frontispiece illustration to a scripture called the* Diamond Sutra *was privately produced in China in 868. It shows the Buddha in discourse with his disciple Subhuti.*

mingled with Daoism, a belief that humans should live in harmony with the natural world, and with Confucianism, which called for social order. Chinese Buddhists came to believe that, after they died, they went to a "pure land" created by a bodhisattva (Buddhist saint) called Amitabha. Similar beliefs developed in Japan, the land of the Shinto religion.

Temples and Monasteries

Buddhist temples were not used for communal acts of worship, although they housed statues and images that were venerated by the faithful. Many temples were places of pilgrimage or centers of religious festivals. They were often used as storehouses of Buddhist scriptures. Building and providing support for temples was seen as an "act of merit," a noble deed that would help an individual achieve enlightenment.

Some city temples included accommodation for communities of monks or nuns. Monasteries were also founded in remote landscapes, by mountains or lakes, where solitude encouraged meditation.

Cultural Legacy

Medieval Buddhism had an enduring cultural impact wherever it thrived. In architecture, for example, the sacred stupa of India, a dome-shaped Buddhist shrine, evolved in China into a pagoda, a slender, multistoried tower with projecting roofs.

Large statues of the Buddha were carved into rock faces in Afghanistan and China. Smaller statues were made from pottery or bronze. Mandalas (circular paintings), produced by Tibetan monks, were used to aid meditation, as were chanting and music.

The distribution of sutras, deemed an act of merit, motivated the development of the world's first woodblock printing in China and Korea; the printing of Buddhist texts dates to the early years of the eighth century.

Burgundy

THE MEDIEVAL DUKES OF BURGUNDY ruled over an ancient kingdom in the valleys of the Rhône and Saône Rivers (in present-day eastern France and southwestern Germany). At the height of their power, in the fourteenth and fifteenth centuries, their territory also covered the wealthy cloth-producing lands of Flanders (present-day Belgium and Holland). During this period the dukes of Burgundy played a key role in regional politics, and the Burgundian court became a thriving center of European culture.

The Kingdom of Burgundy

The people the Romans knew as Burgundians were perhaps originally a Scandinavian people who began moving southward and westward in the first century CE. They established a powerful kingdom around the Rhine River (in present-day Germany) that gradually spread west. By the fifth century Burgundian terri-

tory covered present-day Switzerland and had reached the Rhône and Saône valleys. The Burgundian kingdom remained independent until 534, when it was conquered by the Franks. After this conquest, control of Burgundy passed first to the Merovingian kings of the Franks and then to Charles Martel, mayor of the East Frankish kingdom, and his grandson, Charlemagne.

▶ *This map shows the remarkable growth of the kingdom of Burgundy between 1400 and 1492.*

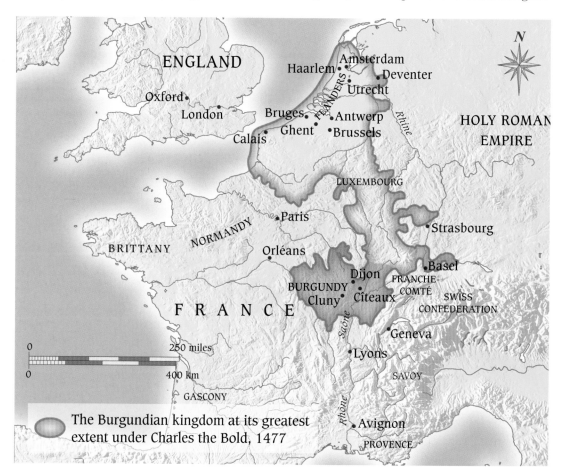

The Burgundian kingdom at its greatest extent under Charles the Bold, 1477

BURGUNDIAN ABBEYS

Two great monastic orders of the Middle Ages had roots in the territory of Burgundy. At the influential Benedictine abbey of Cluny, founded in 910, the the Cluniac variant of Benedict's Rule was founded. The Cistercian order was named after the abbey founded at Cîteaux in 1098. One of the monks of Cîteaux, later Saint Bernard of Clairvaux, was instrumental in spreading Cistercian ideas.

Following the death of Charlemagne in 814, the kingdom of Burgundy was divided several times between different rulers, but by the eleventh century it had become two distinct entities. The western part, known as the Duchy of Burgundy, was theoretically subject to the king of France, while the eastern part, called the County of Burgundy, or Franche-Comté, was part of the Holy Roman Empire.

The Rise of the Duchy

In the mid-thirteenth century the Duchy of Burgundy was conquered by King Louis VIII of France as part of his conquest of the south of the country. It was subsequently given to one of the French king's sons and was passed on to his descendants. The last of this line, Duke Philip of Rouvres, died in 1361 without leaving an heir, and so the duchy returned to the French king's control. In 1364 King John II of France made his youngest son, Philip, the new duke of Burgundy; this new line of Valois dukes would rule until 1477.

In 1369 Duke Philip the Bold, as he became known, acquired through marriage the territories of Flanders and Franche-Comté for the duchy. The next two dukes continued this policy of gaining land until by the 1440s the duchy stretched from central France to the North Sea. Under the Valois dukes (1364–1477), Burgundy became extremely wealthy. Its farmers produced high-quality grain, wine, and wool, and the cities of Flanders were wealthy centers of cloth making and banking.

▲ *The consecration of a Cluniac abbey by Pope Urban II is depicted in this twelfth-century manuscript.*

CHRONOLOGY

1ST CENTURY CE
Burgundians begin to settle in the Rhine valley.

534
The kingdom of Burgundy is conquered by Franks.

1000s
Burgundy becomes two separate territories: Duchy of Burgundy and Franche-Comté.

1364–1477
Burgundy is ruled by Valois dukes: Philip the Bold, John the Fearless, Philip the Good, and Charles the Bold.

1369
Duke Philip the Bold marries Margaret of Flanders.

1476
Marie of Burgundy marries Maximilian Hapsburg.

1477–1493
France and Austria fight over Burgundy.

1493
The Treaty of Senlis divides Burgundy between France and Austria.

1556
Franche-Comté and Flanders become part of the Spanish Hapsburg Empire.

1648
Flanders becomes independent.

1678
Franche-Comté becomes part of France.

Quarrels and Wars

By the 1400s the dukes of Burgundy were among the most powerful nobles at the court of the king of France. Their power enticed them into constant battles with their rivals, the dukes of Orléans and their supporters, the Armagnacs. Later the Burgundian dukes quarreled with Charles VI's eldest son, known as the dauphin. In 1419 Duke John the Fearless of Burgundy was assassinated, probably on the dauphin's orders, and afterward the duchy supported England against France in the second phase of the conflict known as the Hundred Years War (1337–1453).

Divided Lands

In 1476 Duke Charles the Bold of Burgundy arranged for his only child, Marie, to marry Prince Maximilian Hapsburg of Austria, the heir to the Holy Roman Empire. However, the following year Charles died in battle, and King Louis XI of France seized some of his lands. For the next seventeen years Maximilian fought the French over Burgundy. Finally, in the Treaty of Senlis of 1493, Maximilian agreed with the French king, Charles VIII, to divide Burgundy between them, with the western part of the duchy joining France, while Franche-Comté and Flanders became part of the Austrian Hapsburg Empire.

For the following sixty years Franche-Comté and Flanders were ruled by the Austrian Hapsburgs, and in 1556 they passed to the Spanish Hapsburgs. By 1648 Flanders had won its independence from Spain, but Franche-Comté remained a Spanish possession until 1678, when it became part of France.

▲ The Virgin of Autun, *by Jan van Eyck. The kneeling figure on the left is Chancellor Rolin, a leading figure in the Burgundian court.*

SEE ALSO

• Capetians

• Flanders

• France

• Hapsburgs

• Holy Roman Empire

Byzantine Empire

THE BYZANTINE EMPIRE, situated in Asia Minor and the southern Balkan Peninsula, was the eastern part of the Roman Empire. It survived for more than a thousand years after the collapse of the western part. The emperors and their subjects thought of themselves as Romans; the name Byzantine Empire was a term devised by later historians. It derives from Byzantium, the city that Constantine the Great chose as his new capital in 330 CE and that he renamed Constantinople (it is now called Istanbul). At its largest extent the empire's territories included most of the Middle East, Sicily, and southern Italy and part of North Africa.

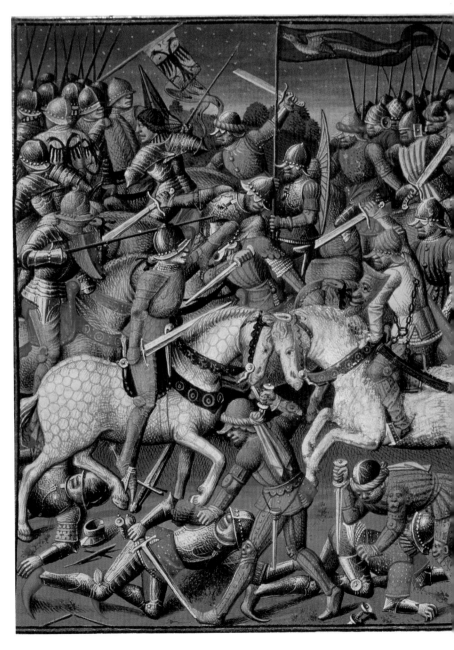

▼ This thirteenth-century painting shows Emperor Heraclius victorious in battle. When Heraclius came to the throne, the Byzantine Empire was under attack from many sides, but his armies were successful at repelling the empire's enemies.

A Divided Empire

What was to become the Byzantine Empire dates from the reign of the first emperor Constantine (306–337), who rebuilt the ancient city of Byzantium as his splendid new capital, Constantinople. Later, when Emperor Theodosius died in 395, the Roman Empire was formally divided into an eastern and a western part, each ruled by one of his sons. In 410 Rome was sacked by Ostrogoth invaders, to whom the Western Empire fell in 476.

The Eastern Empire sought to save itself from a similar fate by enacting various reforms. The office of emperor was made hereditary to avoid disputes over succession, and civil and military authority was separated to make it harder to organize rebellions. An elaborate bureaucracy that regulated virtually all commercial activity in the empire was put in place. Peasants on the land and craftsmen in the workshop alike felt its heavy hand.

War and Conflict

From 610 to 1081 the Byzantine Empire suffered near-continuous assault. The Persians attacked in 610 and threatened to occupy its eastern provinces. In the late

620s Emperor Heraclius routed the Persians and the Avars. For the next 450 years the empire battled Arabs and Bulgars. By 642 the Arabs had conquered Palestine, Syria, and Egypt.

Constantly threatened with invasion, the empire was kept on a permanent war footing. Heraclius introduced the *theme* system, which recombined the civil and military authorities and strengthened the empire's defenses. Each *theme* (an army unit) was settled in a particular region (also called a *theme*) run by a general. The soldiers received allotments of land and so were able to work on their farms and still be available to fight invaders when required.

Under the Macedonian dynasty (867–1025), the Byzantine armies regained large areas of land from the Arabs and the Bulgars, and the empire enjoyed a resurgence of power. However, in the eleventh century, as the *theme* system began to break

down, it became clear that the Byzantine Empire lacked the military strength to continue fighting off its enemies.

Religious Controversy

For more than a century the question of whether or not icons (painted images of Christ and the saints) should be used in worship was hotly debated. In 730 Emperor Leo III ordered all icons destroyed. Monks, the major supporters of icons as aids to prayer, suffered violent persecution for defending them. Despite papal and popular support for icons, only in 843 did the emperor restore them to their honored place in Byzantine Christian life.

Decline and Fall

Around the year 1100 Emperor Alexius I Comnenus tried to restore the economic fortunes of the empire by allowing Venetian merchants to trade in many Byzantine

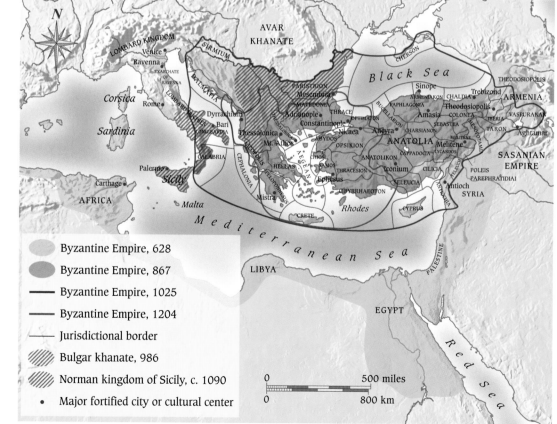

▶ *A map showing the extent and internal divisions of the Byzantine Empire between 628 and 1204.*

Byzantine Empire, 628
Byzantine Empire, 867
Byzantine Empire, 1025
Byzantine Empire, 1204
Jurisdictional border
Bulgar khanate, 986
Norman kingdom of Sicily, c. 1090
• Major fortified city or cultural center

JUSTINIAN I *REIGNED 527–565*

Justinian became emperor upon his uncle's death. He continued the long-standing struggle against the Persians in the east and regained certain former Roman provinces in the west, including North Africa and parts of Italy. He and his flamboyant empress, Theodora, achieved fame for producing a collection of laws, the Code of Justinian (529–565), and for initiating an extensive program of public building, including the magnificent Church of Hagia Sophia.

towns without paying any taxes. Although the towns bustled with commercial activity, most of the profits were extracted by the Italian traders without actually benefiting the Byzantine economy.

Several foreign powers took advantage of the weakened Byzantine Empire. The Pechenegs, a Turkic people from central Asia, invaded the Balkans repeatedly during the eleventh century; the Normans completed their conquest of Italy in 1071; and the empire lost most of Asia Minor to the Turks by the 1090s. From the end of the eleventh century, crusaders began attacking the empire and plundering its wealth.

In 1204 the soldiers of the Fourth Crusade sacked Constantinople and established the Latin Empire of Constantinople. The exiled Byzantines reconquered the city in 1261. By this time, however, their empire had become extremely weak; it faced threats from both western Europeans and the Turks. Constantinople had been reduced to a city-state in the midst of several independent provinces.

By the fourteenth century it had become clear that the Turks would eventually defeat the Byzantine Empire. In 1355 Emperor John V appealed to the pope in Rome for help. However, no assistance was

▲ *Emperor Justinian, surrounded by his court, from a fourteenth-century Latin manuscript. The law code that Justinian produced gathered all Roman law into one place—a remarkable achievement. The Code of Justinian became the foundation of law in most western European countries.*

CHRONOLOGY

324
Byzantium is rebuilt by Constantine and renamed Constantinople.

391
All pagan worship is banned by Theodosius.

395
The Roman Empire is divided into eastern and western parts.

476
The fall of Romulus Augustulus marks the end of the Western Roman Empire.

527–565
Justinian I reigns.

610
Heraclius introduces the *theme* system.

690s
Arabs conquer Byzantine North Africa.

730
Emperor Leo III orders the destruction of icons.

813
A Byzantine army defeats the Bulgars.

843
Use of icons is once again permitted.

1054
The Orthodox Church is born as it separates from the Roman Catholic Church because of doctrinal disputes.

1204
Constantinople falls to crusaders during the Fourth Crusade.

1261
Exiled Byzantines retake Constantinople.

1453
Constantinople falls to the Ottoman Turks; the Byzantine Empire comes to an end.

offered by the western European Christians, because the Byzantine church had split from the Roman church in 1054.

In 1422 Ottoman forces laid siege to Constantinople. In 1439 Emperor John VIII and his bishops, hoping for western assistance, agreed that the Byzantine church would submit to Rome's authority. The Turks finally took Constantinople on May 29, 1453, and proceeded to murder much of the civilian population and destroy artifacts that had survived for a millennium. The last emperor, Constantine XI, died fighting on the city walls.

Life for Ordinary People

There was little contact between the literate, Greek-speaking Byzantine rulers and the people of their empire, the vast majority of whom were peasants who worked the land using techniques that had advanced little since ancient times. Every year peasants were visited by tax collectors accompanied by soldiers. Those who failed to pay had their goods taken and were flogged.

Byzantine society also made great use of slaves. From the ninth to the eleventh centuries, when the empire achieved a number of military victories, enemy soldiers seized in battle were forced to work as slaves for the wealthy.

Most of Constantinople's inhabitants were very poor and typically lived in small huts with little access to sanitation. Occasionally the poor rioted to protest the squalor of their living conditions.

Achievements and Legacy

Throughout most of the Byzantine period, Constantinople was a city of splendor far in

▼ A sixteenth-century fresco showing the siege of Constantinople. The Turks looted the city for three days after overpowering it. Constantinople was renamed Istanbul and became the new capital of the Ottoman Empire.

Christianity was the official religion of the empire, but only in its last few centuries was the majority of the empire's population Christian. In rural areas many people converted to Christianity, but the old pagan rituals and superstitions remained alive throughout the early period of Byzantine rule. Pagan customs gradually became incorporated into popular Christianity. There were also many Jewish people scattered throughout the empire, mainly in the cities. Jews were allowed to practice their religion but were barred from certain jobs and suffered other indignities.

▲ *An early-eleventh-century mosaic of Christ. In late-Roman art, important religious figures were shown with a halo.*

advance of the greatest western European cities of the time. It boasted luxurious royal palaces, the magnificent Hagia Sophia cathedral, public baths, and a class of scholars who were learned in the writings of classical Greece and Rome.

The Byzantine Empire continued the traditions of Greek culture and developed high standards of art and architecture. Byzantine art, Christian in content and purpose, portrayed the lives of Jesus and the saints. The Byzantines adapted Roman techniques in the building of their churches and basilicas, although in later times their designs became more ornate.

Other aspects of Byzantine culture were somewhat stagnant, however. Byzantine literature lacked originality, as it tended to imitate styles from the classical era. Developments in science were limited, and

most thinkers, accepting the biblical understanding of the physical world, believed, for example, that the world was flat rather than round. There were few advances in agriculture or in military strategy or technology.

Nevertheless, some technological progress was made—in the silk industry and in paper making, for example. The Byzantines also adopted the latest mechanical developments, including cogwheels, screws, and pulleys, in their manufacturing processes.

The Byzantine Empire was notable for its success in fending off enemies and its ability to revive after periods of disaster. During the centuries when learning was at its lowest ebb in western Europe, Byzantine society succeeded in preserving the heritage of ancient Greece and Rome.

SEE ALSO

Calendars and Clocks

FOR MOST PEOPLE living in the early Middle Ages, the precise measurement of dates and hours—a state of affairs now taken for granted—was unimportant. A lunar calendar might be used to calculate religious festivals. The accurate measurement of solar time—a year being the length of time it took for the sun to go around the earth—was of secondary interest to ordinary people. Sundials, candles, sandglasses, water clocks, and the time it took to sing certain prayers were methods used to measure the passing of time. By the end of the medieval period, however, printed calendars were in wide distribution, and in 1582 the existing calendar was adjusted to make it more accurate. Meanwhile, the invention of the mechanical clock around 1300 initiated a very different attitude toward time.

▶ *A beautifully illuminated late-fifteenth-century French book of hours. A book of hours was a prayer book used by wealthy nobles that also served as a type of calendar. It included prayers for different times of the day and showed the saints' days and months of the year.*

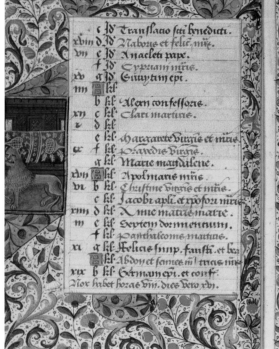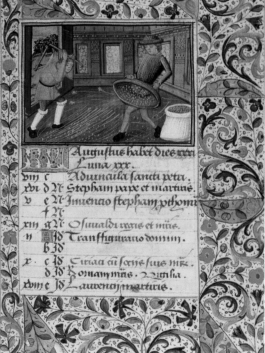

Measuring the Years

The people of western Europe inherited the Julian calendar from the Romans. This calendar, instituted by Julius Caesar in 46 BCE, was modified by later emperors, as well as by the fourth-century Christian historian Eusebius. Finally, in 525 CE an Italian abbot named Dionysius Exiguus adjusted the calendar so that it reckoned water clocks, candles, and even certain elaborate prayers were used to calculate the night hours, although clearly these were not very accurate measures. Some elaborate devices were invented. In China incense clocks emitted different smells to mark the changing times of day, while Arabian craft workers created water clocks with built-in alarms.

▼ *This angel holding a sundial was carved in the mid-twelfth century and stands in the main entrance of the Cathedral of Notre Dame, Paris, France.*

the passage of time from Christ's birth. His method of dating (using the formula "anno Domini," or "in the year of Our Lord") was gradually adopted across the Christian world. The Islamic calendar was calculated from the date of the Hegira, the flight of the prophet Muhammad from Mecca (622).

Adjusting the Calendar

The Julian calendar, whatever its starting point, did not measure the solar year accurately enough, and by the 1500s it had lost about ten days. In 1267 an English friar named Roger Bacon urgently appealed to the pope to set time right, as the Christmas and Easter festivals were no longer being celebrated at the correct time. Bacon's appeal was not acted on, but as time passed, many other clerics expressed concern. In the late 1570s Pope Gregory XIII set up a committee of astronomer monks to adjust the calendar. In 1582 ten days were "removed" from the month of October, and an improved method of calculating leap years was introduced. The Gregorian calendar is still followed.

Measuring the Hours

Until the fourteenth century, people used methods for measuring time that had been developed in the ancient world. Sundials were most commonly used, but they could be read only in bright sunlight. Sandglasses,

THE CANONICAL HOURS

Before clocks were built, monks, nuns, and even village priests followed a routine of regular prayer times, or *horae*, which are known as the canonical hours and were marked by the ringing of bells. While most uneducated people would not have been able to identify every one of the canonical hours, the more educated and richer members of the laity could follow a pattern similar to that of monks and priests, praying at regular intervals during the day, perhaps at services held by their own chaplain.

▲ *This thirteenth-century mechanism, made for the tower clock of Salisbury Cathedral, in Wiltshire, England, is the oldest surviving mechanical timekeeper in Europe.*

Early Clocks

Around 1300 the first mechanical clocks were built. They were driven by a pair of weights and contained an escapement mechanism, which allowed the weights to rise up again and so keep in constant motion. At first, clocks simply chimed the hours, but in 1344 the clock face was invented by Jacopo de Dondi. These early clocks had a single hour hand and a large face that was divided into twenty-four hours. They were placed in church towers so everyone could see them, and they chimed every hour or even every quarter hour. By the fifteenth century most towns had their own clocks.

The next important development in clock making was the spring mechanism, which was first used around 1430. Spring-mechanism clocks were driven by the gradual uncoiling of a cord or chain and could be much smaller than weight-driven clocks. Clock makers created chamber clocks, which were small enough to stand in a room. Alarm clocks were also developed around this time.

A New Attitude to Time

With the invention of the mechanical clock, people became aware of hours for the first time. Merchants could arrange meetings, shops could open at a regular time, and manufacturers could run their business more efficiently. All these changes caused a quickening of the pace of life but also made life in the towns run more smoothly. By the fifteenth century printed calendars were widely available and helped merchants, traders, and bankers to plan ahead.

SEE ALSO
• **Astronomy** • **Bede**

Canute

CANUTE, WHOSE NAME is also spelled Cnut and Knud, was born in Denmark to King Svein Forkbeard and his wife, Sigfrid. Canute (c. 994–1035) assisted his father in the conquest of England, and after the defeat of the Anglo-Saxons, Canute acquired a large empire that covered England, some of the Scottish isles, and Scandinavia.

Invasion

At the time of Canute's birth, England was made up of various territories, some inhabited mainly by Anglo-Saxons and others by Scandinavians—mainly Danes—who had migrated there. In 1000 the Anglo-Saxon king, Aethelred, attacked the Isle of Man and the Danelaw, a swath of land covering parts of northern, eastern, and central England. Aethelred feared that the Danish population of these areas was likely to rise against the Anglo-Saxons, and in 1002 he ordered a massacre of the Danish population in England. According to later medieval stories, one of the victims was Canute's aunt, the sister of Svein Forkbeard. If true, it may be that a desire for revenge led Svein to invade England in 1003. Svein sailed to England to avenge his countrymen's deaths. He carried out several raids on the English coast, and in 1013 he decided to conquer England. Canute, now a young man, accompanied Svein on the campaign.

English resistance collapsed in the face of a massive Danish attack, and Aethelred fled to Normandy. When Svein died a few months later, Aethelred siezed the chance to regain his lost kingdom and succeeded in driving out the Danes, now under Canute's command. As the Danish army prepared to sail back to Denmark, Canute cut off the hands, ears, and noses of his father's prisoners and set them ashore at Sandwich in

Kent as a warning to the Anglo-Saxons that he would return.

Conquest

The Danes helped Canute amass a huge army and two hundred ships, each one carrying eighty men. In 1015 he returned to England. After prolonged fighting, culminating in the battle of Ashingdon (1016), Canute brought Aethelred's heir, Edmund Ironside, to the brink of defeat. Edmund and Canute signed a treaty at Olney. Canute became ruler of the Danelaw and the midlands, while Ironside kept control of southern England.

▲ In this illustration from a fourteenth-century manuscript, King Canute is depicted seated on his throne. Legend has it that he once placed his crown on a crucifix at Winchester Cathedral to show his subjects that God was the only true ruler.

anute was a religious man and an astute politician. According to a centuries-old tale, when he learned that his courtiers were boasting that he was so great he could command the tide to turn back, he decided to teach them a lesson. He had his throne brought to the seashore, and seating himself there, he commanded the waves to leave the shore. When they did not, he declared: "Let all men know how empty and worthless is the power of kings. For there is none worthy of the name but God, whom heaven, earth, and sea obey." With these words Canute impressed his subjects with his humility and also showed them that kings do not always get what they—or their courtiers—wish for.

Canute's Reign

Canute was a Christian, and he felt guilty for having killed so many in battle. He tried to atone for his sins by building churches in England and Denmark. He also sent missionaries to Scandinavia and undertook a pilgrimage to Rome. Under Canute's rule the empire prospered. For nearly twenty years peace between England and Scandinavia allowed trade and the arts to flourish. Canute taxed his subjects heavily, but they were grateful for the peace and order he brought, and he was remembered as a just ruler. After Canute's death, the English and Danish thrones passed to his sons. They were ineffective rulers, and the empire soon broke up.

SEE ALSO
• **Denmark** • **England** • **Vikings**

▲ To atone for the bloodshed he caused, King Canute often donated lavish gifts to the churches in England.

When Ironside died shortly afterward, Canute inherited his part of the kingdom. In 1019 Canute's brother Harald died also, and Canute inherited the Danish crown. Canute later annexed Norway (1028) and Sweden (c. 1030) to his empire.

Capetians

THE CAPETIAN DYNASTY, named after its founder, Hugh Capet, ruled France for 341 years, from 987 until 1328. The Capetians extended the power of the monarchy, created a centralized administrative system, and curbed the independence of the great lords. Under the Capetians, France was transformed from a feudal society to a nation-state.

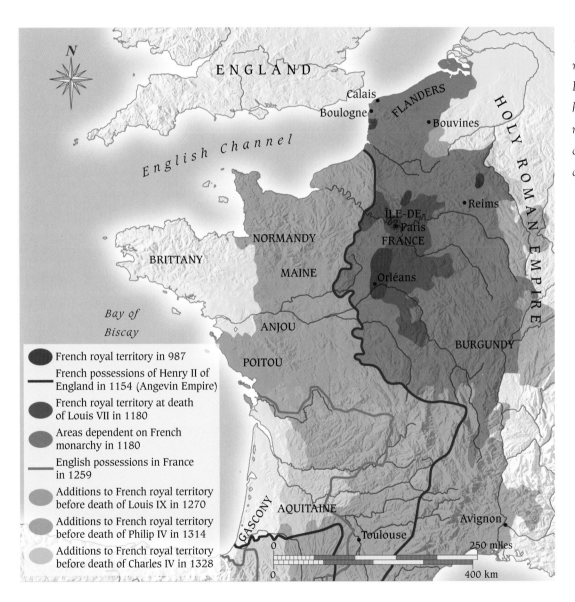

With the growth of royal power under Philip II Augustus and his successors, more and more French territory came under the direct control of the king.

Map legend:
- French royal territory in 987
- French possessions of Henry II of England in 1154 (Angevin Empire)
- French royal territory at death of Louis VII in 1180
- Areas dependent on French monarchy in 1180
- English possessions in France in 1259
- Additions to French royal territory before death of Louis IX in 1270
- Additions to French royal territory before death of Philip IV in 1314
- Additions to French royal territory before death of Charles IV in 1328

Map labels: ENGLAND, Calais, Boulogne, FLANDERS, Bouvines, English Channel, HOLY ROMAN EMPIRE, Reims, ÎLE-DE-FRANCE, Paris, NORMANDY, BRITTANY, MAINE, Orléans, Bay of Biscay, ANJOU, BURGUNDY, POITOU, GASCONY, AQUITAINE, Avignon, Toulouse

Scale: 0 — 250 miles / 0 — 400 km

Founding a Dynasty

In 987 Louis V, the last king of the Carolingian dynasty, died with no male heir. The leading nobles and churchmen offered the crown to Hugh Capet, count of Paris, who held a small area of land around Paris and Orléans called the Île-de-France.

At the time France was made up of counties and duchies whose lords were often richer and more powerful than the king. These lords were expected to swear an oath of loyalty to the king. They were willing to do so because it gave legitimacy to their rule and provided a good example

The tomb effigies of the last Capetian king, Charles IV, and his queen, Jeanne, who are buried in the Basilica of Saint Denis near Paris.

THE CAPETIAN DYNASTY

987–996	Hugh Capet
996–1031	Robert II the Pious
1031–1060	Philip I
1060–1108	Louis VI the Fat
1137–1180	Louis VII
1180–1223	Philip II Augustus
1223–1226	Louis VIII
1226–1270	Louis IX (Saint Louis)
1270–1285	Philip III
1285–1314	Philip IV the Fair
1314–1316	Louis X
1316–1322	Philip IV
1322–1328	Charles IV

to their own followers. In fact, the early Capetian kings had little real power over the lords. The Capetian line was secured by the ingenious policy of crowning the eldest son as a coruler during the king's lifetime.

The Angevins

In the middle of the twelfth century, Capetian rule was threatened by the rise of the Angevins, the counts of Anjou. In 1154 Henry of Anjou, who already held much of western France, inherited the crown of England as Henry II and became the most powerful ruler in Europe.

The Angevin challenge was met by Philip II Augustus (reigned 1180–1223), a skillful politician driven by the single-minded aim of increasing French royal power. Perceiving the bitter family quarrels within the Angevin family, Philip encouraged Henry's sons to rebel against their father and then set brother against brother.

Philip's Conquests

While the second Angevin king of England, Richard I, was away fighting a Crusade, Philip began to seize the English territories in France. After Richard's death, which came fighting to regain his French lands, Philip went to war with Richard's brother and successor, King John, and conquered Normandy in 1204.

Philip faced his greatest challenge in 1214, when an alliance was formed against him by John, the emperor of Germany, and the counts of Flanders and Boulogne. Philip met and defeated them in battle at Bouvines. A third of France was now under direct royal control.

Priest Kings

Capetian prestige came from the rulers' claim to have an authority similar to that of

▲ *King Louis IX, with a saint's halo, sets off on his second and last Crusade, in March 1270. The following August he would die of an infection near Tunis, murmuring, "Oh Jerusalem! Oh Jerusalem!"*

PHILIP THE FAIR REIGNED 1285–1314

Philip IV, known as "the Fair" for his good looks, was so self-confident that he believed that anyone who opposed him was an enemy of God. In 1303, after quarreling with Pope Boniface VIII, Philip accused the pope of heresy and threatened to put him on trial. When Boniface's successor died in 1304, Philip used his influence to have a Frenchman elected pope. The new pope, Clement V, who moved the papal residence from Rome to Avignon in southern France, was widely considered a tool of the French king.

In October 1307 Philip destroyed the crusading order of the Knights Templar. All the Templars in France were arrested and accused of crimes, including the worshiping of idols and spitting on the cross. Philip may have believed these charges, which were almost certainly false, or merely used them as an excuse to seize the order's wealth. The fact that he was able to destroy the Templars shows how powerful the French king had become.

priests in addition to the simple worldly power of other lords and to derive their right to rule from God. Each king was accorded this special status in an elaborate coronation ceremony at Reims, in northeastern France. During the ceremony the king was anointed with holy oil believed to have been brought down from heaven by a dove. From the eleventh century, Capetian kings also claimed the power to cure a disease called scrofula by touch. On special religious days, such as Easter and Pentecost, people lined up to be touched by the king.

Saint Louis

No king took his religious duties more seriously than Louis IX (reigned 1226–1270), who led two Crusades and who was declared a saint after his death. Louis believed that every act of a king, both in public and private, should follow strict religious principles. On his deathbed he left instructions for his son: "Keep yourself from doing anything that is displeasing to God. . . . Rather than commit such a terrible offence you must on the contrary be ready to suffer every kind of torment."

End of the Dynasty

After Philip the Fair's death in 1314, his three sons ruled in turn, each dying after a short reign without a son to follow him. In 1328, on the death of the third son, the crown passed to his cousin Philip of Valois, who founded a new dynasty. The house of Valois, a branch of the Capetian family, would rule France until 1589.

Captivity and Ransom

THE TREATMENT OF PRISONERS OF WAR varied greatly from one part of the world to another during the Middle Ages. In some societies mercy was rarely shown, and a defeated enemy was generally enslaved or killed. Japanese knights, called samurai, regarded captivity as so shameful that they preferred suicide. In Europe at least the most important captives were usually spared. They would be released when a payment, called a ransom, had been collected from the enemy.

In the tribal societies of Africa, the Americas, and Oceania, warriors might treat captives as their beliefs directed. Torture, the cutting off of heads, and cannibalism were common practices. Even in more-complex societies, religious custom might dictate ritual slaughter of captives to honor the gods. In Aztec Mexico, in 1487, tens of thousands of captured Huaxtec rebels were sacrificed to the god Huitzilopochtli over a period of just four days. From the Aztec point of view, being sacrificed in such a way was deemed a great honor rather than a punishment.

This illustration from 1492 shows Angevin prisoners captured by King Ferdinand II of Aragon being led away.

Religious Wars

A great many wars were fought in the name of religion, yet even followers of those religions that preached compassion showed little mercy to their prisoners. When Christian crusaders captured Jerusalem in 1099, they massacred both Muslims and Jews. Captured Cathars, members of a heretical Christian sect, were burned alive during the Albigensian Crusade in southern France in the early thirteenth century.

Rebels and Traitors

In Europe prisoners of war were rarely imprisoned for a long period of time, unless awaiting trial for an offense such as treason. Such a prisoner's captors would torture him until his body was broken, to gain either a confession or information that would implicate others. He then faced a wretched death. In 1305 the Scottish patriot William Wallace, who was captured by the English, was first hanged. While he was still alive, his organs were cut from his body, which was then torn into four pieces. The severed head of one deemed a traitor was often displayed on a city wall.

Status of Captives

In feudal societies, the life of a common soldier counted for little. However, in later medieval Europe the rules of war decreed mutual respect between the king, nobles, and knights of each side. They were often related to each other and shared a culture that was very different from that of common soldiers. Important prisoners would be detained until a ransom was paid. They would spend their captivity in a castle, under the protection of a royal official called a constable. They might be treated civilly and join their hosts in hunting or feasting.

KINGS' RANSOMS

King Richard I of England was imprisoned by his enemy Leopold, duke of Austria, while returning from the Third Crusade in 1192. Richard was handed over to Leopold's overlord, the Holy Roman Emperor Henry VI, and his release was secured only in 1194 after payment of a ransom of 150,000 marks, equivalent to three years' income for the English king. The crusader king Louis IX of France, captured by the Saracens in 1250, had to surrender an entire city, Damietta (in Egypt), to buy his freedom. The ransom for John II of France, who was captured by the English at Poitiers in 1356, amounted to twice the annual income of his kingdom.

▼ This gold coin was issued in 1360 to pay the English for the ransom of King John II (the Good) of France. John died as a prisoner in London in 1364, before his ransom was fully redeemed.

Payment of Ransoms

Ransoms could take many years to settle and generally took the form of large sums of money, which feudal subjects were obliged to pay. Ransoms could cause great hardship at home, as estates were sold and taxes collected to free a captive lord. A religious order, the Trinitarians, was founded in 1198 with the aim of collecting money to pay ransoms of captured crusaders. Ransom demands led to the increasing commercialization of warfare, with knights seeking profit rather than outright victory.

SEE ALSO
- **Battles**
- **Crime and Punishment**
- **Heresy**
- **Torture**
- **Warfare**

Carolingians

THE CAROLINGIANS RULED the Frankish kingdom from 751 to 987. At the height of their power, they controlled an empire that extended from northern Spain to Poland and Hungary. The family, originally called Arnulfings, after an ancestor named Arnulf, first rose to power in the seventh century. They have long been called Carolingians after the greatest of their rulers, Charlemagne, or Charles the Great—*Carolus magnus* in Latin. The Carolingians oversaw an intellectual and artistic revival, the establishment of feudalism, and the consolidation of Christianity in western Europe.

The First Carolingians

Under the Merovingian dynasty the Frankish crown was in decline. Aristocratic landowners took more and more power from the ineffectual rulers. The constant squabbles of the noble families wasted the king's resources.

Charles Martel, an Arnulfing, held the powerful position of palace mayor in the early eighth century. By 725 he had established himself as effective ruler of the Franks, the king himself being little more than a figurehead. Charles subdued neighboring kingdoms and in 732 defeated the Arabs at the Battle of Tours (also known as the Battle of Poitiers) and halted their expansion into the main part of Europe from the Spanish peninsula. He was so secure in his position as ruler that when King Theuderic IV died in 737, the throne stayed vacant until 743.

The End of Merovingian Rule

Charles Martel died in 741, and his sons Pépin the Short and Carloman took over; when Carloman became a monk in 747, Pépin was left in charge. With the church's approval, Pépin ousted the king in 751 and was crowned in his place. In return for its support, Pépin helped the church in its campaign to prevent the Lombards from extending their territory to include Rome.

Growth of the Empire

Pépin, continuing the strong rule of his father, gained additional neighboring territories and established diplomatic links with Constantinople (present-day Istanbul) and Baghdad. On his death in 768, the kingdom was divided between his two sons, Carloman and Charles (Charlemagne). Carloman died soon after, and the kingdom was united under Charlemagne.

CHRONOLOGY

732
Charles Martel defeats the Arabs at the Battle of Tours.

741
Charles Martel dies.

751
Pépin the Short deposes the last Merovingian king, Childerich III.

800
Charlemagne is crowned Roman emperor by Pope Leo III.

843
Treaty of Verdun divides Carolingian kingdom in three on the death of Louis I.

887
Carolingian rule in Italy ends after the deposition of Charles the Fat.

911
Carolingian rule in Germany ends after Louis the Child dies with no heir.

987
King Louis V of France, the last Carolingian ruler, dies.

◄ *This marble throne in the gallery of the Palatine chapel in Aachen Cathedral may have been used by Charlemagne and was certainly used for the coronation of the later Holy Roman emperors.*

The rule of Charlemagne was the high point of the Carolingian dynasty. Oustanding as both a military leader and diplomatic strategist, Charlemagne continued the extension of Carolingian territory begun by Pépin and cemented relations with the church. In 774 he helped form the Papal States in central Italy and vowed to defend the papacy. By 800 the Carolingian empire covered much of western Europe, and Charlemagne was the most powerful ruler since the emperors of ancient Rome. He had also done much to spread Christianity among pagan peoples. On Christmas Day 800 Pope Leo III crowned him emperor of a renewed Roman empire.

Carolingians from Charlemagne onward presided over a revival of classical and early-Christian learning and styles of art. This renewed interest in the past had a lasting impact on the architecture of Europe. The square, closed shapes favored by the Merovingians were replaced by the vaulting, spacious structures that evolved into the Romanesque style. The best surviving example of Carolingian architecture is the Palatine chapel at Aachen, designed by Odo of Metz and built in 805.

The map shows the Carolingian kingdom after its division under the terms of the Treaty of Verdun (843).

Legal and Social Systems

Under the Carolingians the feudal system became fully established and was applied across the extent of their realm. The Frankish kingdoms had always been wracked by rivalries among powerful aristocratic families. In an attempt to avoid disruption to his own rule, Charlemagne made first the nobles and finally all males over twelve swear an oath of fealty. In exchange for paying tribute and offering service to their ruler, nobles held their lands and offices for the duration of their life.

Laws regulating the feudal oath and relating to religious and civil offenses were laid down in capitularies. These documents formed the basis of a legal system that set out entitlements, restrictions on behavior, and punishments for crimes ranging from human sacrifice to eating meat during Lent.

Christianity

The Carolingians built strong bonds with the church in Rome. With this strategy they strengthened their own power. As anointed kings they had divine legitimacy for their rule, and later, as emperors of a Christian empire and defenders of the papacy, they had a role within the church. Charles Martel encouraged Saint Boniface's Christian missionary activity in the conquered Germanic lands. For him and later Carolingians, the spreading of Christianity helped to unite and consolidate their new territories.

Dividing the Empire

Following the tradition of the Frankish kings, Charlemagne planned to divide the empire between his sons on his death. As two sons died before him, the empire passed down intact to his remaining son, Louis the Pious.

Louis did not share his father's military skills. His efforts were spent on securing the borders against external threats and on trying to resolve internal turmoil caused by his division of the empire between the sons of his first and second marriages. He was more successful in consolidating the church. He ensured that all monasteries followed the Benedictine rule and halted the seizure of church land holdings by the state and nobility.

After Louis's death his sons argued and warred over the division of the kingdom; the problem was finally resolved with the Treaty of Verdun in 843. Most of France went to Charles II (Charles the Bald); the eastern area that roughly corresponds to present-day Germany went to Louis the German; and the middle portion, from the Low Countries to Italy, went to Lothair,

along with the title of emperor. However, Lothair died without an heir, and Charles the Bald became emperor and ruled from 875 until his death in 877.

The lands continued to be further divided and subdivided on the death of successive kings and also eroded by both domestic difficulties and raids by Saracens, Magyars, and Vikings. The empire was briefly reunited by Charles the Fat in 885, but after he was deposed in 887, owing to his failure to combat Viking raids effectively, the empire broke up for good. Carolingian rule ended in France in 987 with the rise to power of the Capetians.

▲ *This illustration of Lothair, the eldest son of Louis the Pious, is part of a manuscript that dates from 1004. Lothair and his brothers overthrew their father and seized power for a brief period in 830 and again in 833.*

SEE ALSO
• **Capetians** • **Charlemagne** • **Feudalism**
• **France** • **Holy Roman Empire**
• **Merovingians**

Castles and Forts

BY THE TENTH CENTURY landowners in Europe had begun building fortified homes for themselves and their soldiers. By the 1200s there were walled stone castles all over Europe. Fortifications were at their strongest in the 1300s, but by the 1400s comfort had become more important than defense. Castle building was mainly restricted to Europe—in the Middle East Muslims built military forts, and Byzantine cities were protected by massive walls. An independent tradition of castle building grew up in Japan.

Early Castles

Castles had to be strong and easy to defend and also had to be spacious to accommodate soldiers and servants, as well as the lord and his family. Some of the earliest castles were known as motte and bailey castles. They had a tall wooden tower built on a mound of earth, called the motte, and a bailey (or courtyard) at the base of the motte. The tower was constantly guarded and provided an excellent lookout point. The people of the castle lived in a cluster of buildings inside the bailey. The motte and bailey were linked by a wooden bridge and surrounded by a high wooden fence. When the castle was attacked, everyone sought shelter in the tower.

Stone Castles

By 1100 castle builders had begun to replace wooden towers with strong stone structures that no longer stood apart on a motte but were surrounded by a walled bailey. Great towers could be square, rectangular, circular, or even octagonal. They contained a large hall for feasting and a

▼ Cardiff Castle in Wales (eleventh century) is one of the few surviving motte and bailey castles. Most motte and bailey castles were built from wood and so have disappeared completely.

comfortable room, known as the solar, for the lord and his family. They also provided accommodation for castle guards and servants. The many other buildings in the bailey included kitchens, stables, and outhouses.

By the thirteenth century most castles no longer had a great tower. Instead builders, concentrating on strengthening the bailey walls, built heavily fortified castles that were influenced by Islamic and crusader forts. The castles featured high curtain walls topped by battlements and pierced by firing loops (narrow slits for shooting arrows).

CRUSADER CASTLES

Crusaders from western Europe were familiar with castles in their homelands. Great stone towers were already being built in Normandy, for example, and hilltop castles in other areas. In the eastern lands they conquered, the crusaders found impressive Byzantine walled cities, the round towers of the Armenians, and Islamic castles. Although they probably drew on all of these styles of military building, they went far beyond them and brought the art of castle building to its peak. The military orders were the great castle builders of the eastern Mediterranean, as can be seen in the fortress of Krak des Chevaliers.

The Islamic style of castle building can be seen in the castles of southern Spain, where castles built by the Muslim Moors use a type of decorative brickwork that is also found in Moorish mosques.

▶ *The fortress of Krak des Chevaliers, in Syria, an outstanding example of an early concentric castle, was built by the crusader Knights of Saint John in the twelfth century.*

CHRONOLOGY

c. 950
First castles are built in Europe.

1000s
Wooden motte and bailey castles are built in Europe.

1096
Crusades begin; meeting of western and eastern styles leads to new developments.

1100s
Stone castles are built across Europe.

c. 1200
Castles without towers become popular.

1270s
First concentric castles are built in Europe.

1300s
First tower castles are built in Japan.

1400s
Castle building in Europe starts to decline.

Watchtowers were built into the castle walls at regular intervals, and many castles were surrounded by a moat. Gatehouses, also known as barbicans, were especially heavily fortified. Over the moat there was often a drawbridge, which was raised when an enemy attacked; an extra metal gate called a portcullis was lowered to keep out enemies.

The highly developed castles of the military orders in the eastern Mediterranean in turn influenced castle building in western Europe. Around 1280 a new style of heavily defended castle, known as a concentric castle, began to be built. It had a double row of bailey walls and relied on water defenses wherever possible. The spacious layout of the castle allowed more space to be devoted to living quarters, with separate suites of rooms for the lord's family and his guests. The multiwalled design of the concentric castle may have been inspired by the triple walls surrounding the city of Constantinople (the capital of the Byzantine Empire).

Building a Castle

Castles were very expensive to build and required careful planning. First, a suitable site had to be chosen. Some castles were built on high ground to allow a good view of any approaching enemies, while others were positioned at important river crossings or to guard frontiers, ports, or cities. Castles had to be close to a good water supply and, if possible, near a quarry and a forest, sources of building materials.

Once a site was chosen, designs were drawn up by a master mason and approved by the castle owner. The master mason then supervised a team of hundreds of workers who dug the foundations, cut stones, mixed up mortar, and laid the stones. Carpenters made wooden scaffolding for the masons to stand on and large wooden tread wheels to winch (hoist) up the stones. The materials were brought to the site on carts, sleds, and wheelbarrows. Castle building sometimes continued right through the winter, but often it stopped during the coldest months, and the tops of the walls would be covered in straw to protect them from frost.

Castles at War

A wide range of military weapons and equipment was developed for use in besieging and defending castles. Besieging armies fired boulders from giant catapults, known

▼ *A 1492 Italian miniature depicting castle construction. Masons are cutting and laying stones, while a winch is being operated above one of the castle walls.*

as mangonels and trebuchets, and charged at castle gates and walls with heavy battering rams. Tall siege towers were wheeled up close to enemy walls to allow soldiers to climb into the castle or attack from close range, while ladders and grappling hooks were used for scaling high walls.

Soldiers defending a castle stood on battlements or hid behind firing loops. Sometimes timber extensions, known as hoardings, were built around a castle's battlements to give the defending archers a better range of fire, but these extensions could be easily smashed or set alight. Circular watchtowers gave defending soldiers the widest possible viewpoint for sighting and attacking the enemy.

NOTABLE CASTLES

A short list of notable castles built during the medieval period in different parts of the world:

Caerphilly, Wales (begun 1277): the first concentric castle in Britain.

Castel del Monte, Italy (begun c. 1240): an eight-sided tower castle.

Friesach, Austria (begun 1077): three early castles, making up a fortified town.

Ghent, Belgium (begun 1177): a European castle directly inspired by the crusader castles.

Himeji, Japan (begun c. 1350): a beautiful tower castle known as the White Heron.

Krak des Chevaliers, Syria (rebuilt late twelfth century): a crusader castle built on the site of a Muslim fort.

La Mota, Spain (rebuilt mid-fifteenth century): a brick castle combining Christian and Moorish styles.

Orford, England (begun c. 1165): a castle with a polygonal great tower.

Defending soldiers shot arrows at their attackers and hurled burning rocks over the battlements. Boiling water was poured though holes, called machicolations, in the base of the battlements or through *meurtrières* (murder holes) in the barbican roof. Enemy soldiers attempting to scale the castle walls were dislodged with long forks or picked up in a giant hook called a crow.

Castle sieges could last for months, and most of them ended in the castle's surrender, as the defending army usually ran out of water or food. Sometimes a besieging army catapulted rotting carcasses into the castle to spread disease or undermined the castle walls by digging tunnels and lighting fires under them.

Castle Life

In times of peace, the lord and lady of the castle and their children lived quietly in their solar and the castle gardens. The children learned to read and write and also played board games, such as chess. The family attended regular services in the castle's chapel.

Part of the lord's role was to entertain his guests by holding lavish feasts and leading hunting and hawking expeditions. Some lords kept a castle jester, while musicians, jugglers, and acrobats were hired to amuse the guests at feasts.

Young boys came to live at the castle to train as knights; they first served as pages and then learned the arts of war from the knights who were living in the castle. Sometimes a tournament was held in the castle grounds, and the lord and his guests watched as the knights displayed their skills in mock battles called jousts.

Running a Castle

Medieval castles required an enormous staff to keep them running smoothly. The constable was in charge of the castle guards, the chamberlain looked after the lord's finances, the estate steward made sure the castle lands were run efficiently,

Magnificent feasts were held in a castle's great hall. This photograph shows the twelfth-century hall at Castle Hedingham in Essex, England.

Japan has its own tradition of castle building. By the fourteenth century Japanese warlords, known as daimyos, were building hilltop tower castles to defend themselves against their fellow warlords. These elaborate structures had a tall central tower with many sloping roofs surrounded by at least three courtyards laid out in a maze to confuse invaders.

Himeji Castle in Kyoto, Japan, was built in the early seventeenth century. Like many other Japanese tower castles, it has a tall central tower surrounded by a maze of courtyards.

and the house steward was responsible for ordering supplies. There were special servants for cleaning and serving at table, and ladies' maids and nurses looked after the lady of the castle and her children.

In the kitchens the chief cook supervised a large number of kitchen staff, from humble kitchen boys to skilled pastry cooks. The pantler was in charge of the pantry, where the food was kept, while the butler ran the buttery, where the beer and wine were stored.

In the bailey grooms, stable boys, kennel hands, falconers, beekeepers, and gardeners all played their part in the running of the castle. Bakers and brewers made the castle's bread and beer, while carpenters, blacksmiths, and fletchers (arrow-makers) had their workshops in the bailey.

The End of the Age of Castles

The increased use of cannons in the 1400s led to the decline of castle warfare. Castles could not be built strong enough to defend against attackers armed with cannons, and wars were increasingly fought on battlefields. Nevertheless, the form of castles continued long after their function had become obsolete. From the sixteenth century, kings and lords modeled their great houses on medieval stone castles with battlements and moats but built them from a fashionable but soft new medium: brick. These castle-palaces were designed for comfort, with glazed windows, many fireplaces, and chimneys. They contained large, well-decorated rooms for entertaining guests and beautiful formal gardens in the bailey.

SEE ALSO
- **Architecture**
- **Sieges**

Cavalry

UNTIL THE FOURTEENTH CENTURY warfare in medieval Asia and Europe was dominated by cavalry (mounted troops). In Asia, where Mongol horsemen conquered vast territories, the emphasis was on long-distance campaigns, mobility, and speed. In Europe, however, the emphasis was on pitched battles using heavily armored mounted knights. Even after the cavalry was largely superseded by newer forms of warfare, military power still depended on these knights, and they were rewarded with land, privileges, and an honored position in society.

▼ This section of the Bayeux Tapestry depicts the mounted escort of Count Guy de Ponthieu in action at the Battle of Hastings, the decisive battle in the Norman conquest of England in 1066.

The horse was first domesticated on the Eurasian steppes about five thousand years ago. Warriors of these open grasslands, such as Scythians and Parthians, became expert riders and mastered the art of archery from horseback. In the classical age, Persian, Greek, and then Roman armies learned the value of using cavalry for speed and mobility, for scouting out the land, and for supporting infantry.

Riders of the Steppes

For most of the Middle Ages, the central Asian steppes continued to be the domain of horseback warrior bands and armies. In the thirteenth century ruthless Mongol armies led by Genghis Khan and his successors swept through Asia. Their armored horses were smaller but more durable than those used in Europe. Mongol warriors wore scale armor and helmets and were armed with bows and swords. Tatars led by the great Timur Lenk (also known as Tamerlane; 1336–1405) conquered lands from Russia to China.

Europe after Rome

In the fifth century the invasion of central Europe by Asian horsemen, the Huns, forced Germanic warriors westward and hastened the breakup of the western Roman Empire. It became increasingly difficult to maintain large armies of well-trained infantry. In the smaller, less stable kingdoms of the early Middle Ages, small groups of knights became the most effective way of dealing rapidly with bands of raiders.

The Age of the Knight

Larger European states, such as the Byzantine Empire and the empire of

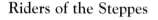

▲ *A 1432 cavalry charge at San Romano in Italy, as painted by Paolo Uccello. The forces of Florence, pitted against Siena's, are led by Niccolò da Tolentino, on the white horse.*

Charlemagne, developed large, well-trained cavalry units. The Norman armies of the eleventh century—invaders of Sicily and the British Isles—achieved territorial control by building castles as regional bases for units of mounted knights.

Norman knights wore armor made of chain mail (interlocking rings of iron). From the 1220s on, knights began to strap protective plates of steel over their mail, and by the start of the fifteenth century, the knight's body was covered entirely by this armor. A knight carried a shield and fought with a lance, long sword, flail, mace, or battle-ax.

THE STIRRUP

One Asian invention that had a major impact on medieval European warfare was the stirrup, used in China from about 400 CE and reaching western Europe by the eighth century. Stirrups, by securing the foot, gave a rider stability and leverage. He could slash down with his sword and absorb impact without being unseated. As a result, the cavalry charge became a formidable strategy.

Training for the charge was provided at mock battles called tournaments. During the jousting event, two knights would charge at each other with lances, each attempting to unseat the other. Tournaments became a sport, often violent and always a grand spectacle.

The Charge

Special warhorses, bred for the richest knights, were much larger and heavier than most riding horses. A heavy cavalry charge inspired fear and awe. The lance was used

A mace made for a wealthy German knight in the 1500s. Maces were heavy clubs used by both infantry and cavalry. A cavalry mace had a shorter handle, with flanges or spikes on its head. Maces appeared in eleventh-century Europe and were widely used by knights through the sixteenth century.

KILLING FIELDS

In order to be certain of success, military planners had to ensure that a heavy-cavalry charge took place on suitable terrain. Conversely, a successful defense against a cavalry charge might be secured by choosing terrain that would make the charge difficult, or by spoiling terrain for mounted riders. In 1244 the Teutonic Knights of Prussia charged the Russians of Novgorod across the frozen waters of Lake Peipus. The ice broke, and the knights were trapped. At Bannockburn in 1314, the English cavalry was cut down in marshy terrain by Scottish infantry arranged in protective schiltrons, small groups of pikemen organized with the pikes pointing outward to ward off cavalry attack. At Agincourt in 1415, a French cavalry charge against the English foundered in the heavy mud of a recently plowed field.

to unseat enemy knights. A dismounted knight could not move quickly, and his visor restricted his field of vision. The momentum of the charge was intended to break the enemy's lines and override its infantry. In the confusion, coats-of-arms, heraldic emblems, and standards helped the knights to identify other combatants.

Fighting the Cavalry

Despite the initial dominance of cavalry, by the fourteenth century a number of countermeasures had brought the military superiority of the cavalry to an end. Infantry defenses against a cavalry charge included pointed stakes set into the ground and metal spikes called caltrops. Long pikes were used to topple riders. Norman crossbows were effective (although they took time to reload). More effective were longbows, developed by the Welsh. The longbow was larger and more powerful than the crossbow, and a good archer could release twelve armor-piercing arrows in a minute. Longbows were used to devastating effect against cavalry during the Hundred

Years War (1337–1453), fought between England and France.

Guns against Horses

By the fourteenth century, gunpowder was taking its toll on the battlefields of Europe. Artillery and, later, handguns, as liable to damage their owner as the enemy, remained unreliable for many years. Nevertheless, firearms eventually brought the age of knights to an end. In 1504 the Spanish defeated the French at Cerignola, near Naples, the first battle to be won by the force of muskets over cavalry (at this stage muskets were light artillery pieces, not the handguns they later became). From the sixteenth century until its final disappearance in the twentieth century, cavalry had to rely on mobility rather than brute force to leave the field victorious.

SEE ALSO
- **Arms and Armor** • **Battles**
- **Hundred Years War** • **Huns** • **Knights**
- **Mongols** • **Tournaments** • **Warfare**

Central Asian Peoples

CENTRAL ASIA IS A VAST REGION that includes the present-day nations of Kazakhstan, Kyrgyzstan, Tajikistan, Turkmenistan, Uzbekistan, and parts of Afghanistan. It has rugged landscapes, extreme weather, dense forests, arid deserts, mighty rivers, and lakes so large as to be inland seas.

A Crossroads of Cultures

In the Middle Ages many different peoples lived in central Asia, including Kazakhs, Kyrgyz, Uzbeks, Turkmen, and Uighurs, who all spoke Turkic languages, and Tadjiks, who spoke Iranian. Each group had its own identity and ambitions, so central Asian people were rarely united. Over the centuries the region became a crossroads of cultures, where many peoples mingled together. It was also the place where rival empires fought for supremacy.

Local Empires

Between 500 and 1000 CE central Asia was ruled by a series of powerful conquerors. Some originated within the region; others were based outside. Leading central Asian powers included two Turkic dynasties: the Ghaznavids, based in Afghanistan, who ruled from 997 to 1186, and the Seljuks, who conquered Ghaznavid territory in 1040 and extended their power west toward Turkey. In eastern central Asia the Uighurs ruled from around 850 to 1218.

Foreign Invaders

Among the most powerful foreign conquerors were Arab armies fighting for Muslim caliphs in Syria and Iraq. They controlled western central Asia from around 700 to 900. The Samanids, from Iran, ruled an empire based in the city of Bukhara from 819 to 1000. However, the most feared of all invaders were Mongols, from northeastern Asia. Under the leadership of Genghis Khan (c. 1162–1227), they conquered all of central Asia between 1218 and 1227.

◀ *Mongol armies with siege engines (front right of picture) surround the redbrick walls of Baghdad (in present-day Iraq) in 1258. Baghdad was the capital of the Abbasid Muslim dynasty. Its capture by the Mongols led to the end of Abbasid power.*

Similar Lifestyles

In spite of their political divisions, central Asian peoples shared similar lifestyles. Living as nomads on steppe grasslands, they tended horses, sheep, and goats. They camped in circular tents, called yurts, made of felt (compressed wool) stretched over wooden frames, and they moved from place to place in search of fresh water and good grazing land. However, in river valleys and on fertile mountain slopes, people lived as farmers in settled villages and went hunting in the forests.

At desert oases and beside long-distance trading routes, central Asian people lived in towns, where they worked as shopkeepers, craftsmen, innkeepers, and money changers. Since the second century BCE, merchants had traveled across central Asia using a network of trackways later known as the Silk Road.

Central Asian Cities

The most important central Asian cities, such as Bukhara and Samarkand, became extremely rich through trade. Their rulers built huge souks (covered markets) and caravanseries (inns where traders, packhorses, and camels could stay). They also paid for magnificent mosques, madrassas (Islamic colleges), palaces, libraries, and tombs. The tomb of Timur, the feared Tatar conqueror, in Samarkand is admired as one of the greatest works of central Asian art. Many cities also became great centers of learning that attracted Muslim scholars, including Ibn Sina (980–1037), known in the West as Avicenna, the greatest scientist of his day.

Artistic Achievements

Central Asian peoples were linked by political conquests, long-distance trade, and a

▶ *This painting, made by a Turkish artist around 1400, depicts Mongol nomads, with their packhorses and hunting dogs, at an overnight camp along the Silk Road.*

CARPET MAKING

Carpet weaving has been part of the everyday life of central Asian peoples for centuries, perhaps even millennia; the oldest surviving pile-knotted rug, found in Pazyryk, eastern Kazakhstan, in 1949, dates from the fifth century BCE. Much of central Asia is mountainous, and the cold winters made floor and bed coverings a necessity. The earliest central Asian carpets were made from wool provided by sheep grazed on the abundant grasslands; later carpet makers picked up silk-weaving skills, passed west from China along the Silk Road. The most commonly found designs are repeating geometric patterns and motifs, some with religious significance.

▼ *This skillfully woven silk tapestry, decorated with pictures of animals, was made in Sogdiana (part of present-day Iran and Afghanistan) around 800.*

shared faith, Islam. Islam was introduced by Arab armies around 650 CE and spread quickly, although minority communities of Buddhists, Christians, Zoroastrians, and Jews also remained.

Islamic ideas, techniques, and designs blended with the many local traditions to create a distinctive central Asian culture. Its achievements included easily portable nomad arts, such as carpets, jewelry, and metalwork, as well as magnificent buildings decorated with patterned brickwork and colored ceramic tiles.

Past and Present

Carpet making and other traditional arts are still practiced in central Asia, and many fine medieval buildings survive. However, central Asia's unsettled past has also left a more troubling heritage of political instability in many parts of the region.

SEE ALSO
• **Genghis Khan** • **Ibn Sina** • **Mongols** • **Seljuk Turks**
• **Silk Road** • **Timur**

CHRONOLOGY

500 CE
Central Asia is divided among nomad tribes (north) and small kingdoms (south).

c. 650–750
Tang Chinese attack from the east.

c. 650–751
Muslim Arabs invade.

c. 700–c. 900
Muslim caliphs rule western central Asia and introduce Muslim culture.

c. 819–1000
Samanids rule an empire based in Bukhara.

977–1186
Ghaznavids rule an empire in southern central Asia and introduce Iranian culture.

c. 1040–1157
Seljuks conquer western central Asia.

c. 1218–1227
The Mongol conquest of central Asia causes much damage but brings peace, which encourages trade.

c. 1370–1405
Timur defeats the Mongols and founds the largest central Asian empire.

c. 1405–1507
Timur's descendants lose control of most of his empire but still encourage central Asian arts.

Chang'an

CHANG'AN, IN WHAT IS NOW SHAANXI PROVINCE, was the Chinese capital under the Sui (581–618 CE) and Tang (618–907) dynasties. At its height in the eighth century, Chang'an was the largest city on earth, with a population of a million within its walls and perhaps another million living in suburbs outside. It was so impressive that its grid plan was copied across eastern Asia. Chang'an provided a model for Kyongju, capital of the Silla kingdom of Korea; Longquanfu, a capital of the Bohai kingdom northeast of China; and the Japanese capitals Nara and Kyoto. The modern-day city of Xi'an is located on the site of Chang'an.

▼ *Yang Chien, who reigned as Emperor Wen Ti and founded Chang'an, is depicted here in a detail from a scroll showing thirteen emperors, painted by Yen Li-Pen, the leading court artist of the Tang dynasty.*

Chang'an was built in the 580s by Wen Ti, the founder of the Sui dynasty, who reunified China after almost four hundred years of division. Wen Ti chose a site close to the capital of the previous rulers of a united China, the Han dynasty (206 BCE–220 CE). The Han capital was also called Chang'an, which means "eternal peace."

The city's location was chosen by using feng shui, the ancient Chinese form of geomancy (divination by interpreting the landscape). It was based on the discovery of lines of energy, called chi, which were believed to flow through the earth and which could bring good fortune. According to feng shui, the ideal place to live has a hill or mountain to the north and a river to the east. The hill was thought to generate chi, which was captured by the river and benefited anyone living in between. The site for Chang'an was chosen because of the Longshou Mountain to the north and the Ba River to the east.

Grid Design

Chang'an was designed as a rectangle enclosing an area of thirty-two square miles (84 km^2). Its grid of streets divided the city into 109 enclosed residential areas called *fang* (wards). The palace stood on the north side at the end of a wide avenue running down the center of the city. This avenue led to the main city gate in the south, the direction linked with good luck.

▼ *This entrance gate of Chang'an's Great Mosque, founded in 742, was built by the Ming emperors in the early 1600s.*

Prosperity and Trade

Chang'an was at its most prosperous under the Tang dynasty. Unlike previous Chinese rulers, the Tang emperors welcomed foreigners, who settled in Chang'an in large numbers. There were Japanese, Koreans, Tibetans, Indians, Persians, Arabs, Jews, and Syrian Christians, each group living in its own ward. The city had two Christian churches, at least one Christian monastery, a Muslim mosque, four Zoroastrian shrines, and dozens of Buddhist and Taoist temples and monasteries.

Chang'an was a great trading center; goods from all over Asia reached its two huge markets, having been carried along a network of roads and canals. It had many beauty spots, featuring gardens and ponds.

During the eighth century, tea drinking was spread by Buddhist monks from southern China, and tea rapidly became the most popular drink throughout the country.

IBN WAHAB, AN ARAB WHO VISITED CHANG'AN IN 881, WROTE A DESCRIPTION OF THE CITY:

The city is of enormous size, with a large population. A long and wide thoroughfare divides the city into two parts. In the east part reside the emperor, ministers, armed forces, supreme judges, and eunuchs, as well as royal retainers. The commoners do not mingle with these people.

QUOTED IN VICTOR CUNRUI XIONG, SUI-TANG CHANGAN

Around the markets of Chang'an were many teahouses, where people relaxed over the fashionable new drink.

Later Chang'an

With the fall of the Tang dynasty in 907, Chang'an lost its position as capital. Yet the city remained an important trading center and revived under the Ming dynasty (1368–1644). The Ming built new city walls and also rebuilt many of Chang'an's buildings.

SEE ALSO

• China

• Cities and Towns

• Silk Road

• Tang Dynasty

Charity

CHARITY HAD A MUCH BROADER MEANING in the Middle Ages than it does now. One of the three principal Christian virtues (the other two being faith and hope), charity was generally interpreted as love of God; it also meant love of others for the sake of God. Charity was the supreme virtue, more important than faith and hope. Its expression in the Middle Ages could take forms that may be recognized as charity in the modern sense—giving alms to the poor, giving to the church, and helping the needy—but the underlying aim of charity was to perfect the charitable individual's relationship with God, not merely to materially benefit the poor or needy who were its objects.

▼ *A representation of the figure of Charity by Giotto di Bondone in a fresco made in 1306.*

In the Middle Ages virtues were often divided into those that can be acquired and those that come as a gift from the Holy Spirit, the latter called "infused," or theological, virtues. Faith, hope, and charity were the three theological virtues.

The idea that virtues could be acquired derives from the teachings of Aristotle. He argued that good moral habits led one to acquire virtues and bad habits led to vices. Aristotle's teachings were reworked by Saint Thomas Aquinas (1225–1274) to fit with the teachings of the Bible.

Thomas Aquinas and Charity

Later-medieval thought about virtue owed a lot to the teachings of Thomas Aquinas. He emphasized charity as the main virtue, calling it the root and end of all other virtues; it could not be attained by the individual's own works alone, however, as it had to be inspired by the Holy Spirit. A life spent acting virtuously would not earn salvation, according to Aquinas, if charity were not present. On the other hand, a single supreme act inspired by charity could wipe out all sin.

The notion that charity is the most important virtue and is the gift of God led to some difficult philosophical problems, such as whether a heathen (a nonbeliever, one not inspired by the Holy Spirit) could ever be truly virtuous and so be saved from damnation.

Charity and Cupidity

For the medieval theologians, charity was the manifestation of love. It was love of God, love for others (even enemies and sinners), and love for oneself. However, by saying that charity is love, theologians and philosophers left room for confusion and error. They had to distinguish between charity and cupidity, meaning sexual desire, romantic love, or any other kind of love that seeks some benefit. A fine line separates virtuous love from sinful love, a line that inspired much art and literature. For example, a poet might describe his love for a woman in terms usually associated with praise for the Blessed Virgin, or he might assert the purity of his love in an attempt to distance it from lust.

THROUGHOUT THE MIDDLE AGES THE WRITINGS OF SAINT AUGUSTINE OF HIPPO (354–430) REMAINED INFLUENTIAL. HE DISTINGUISHED BETWEEN LOVING OTHERS FOR GOD'S SAKE (CHARITY) AND LOVING OTHERS FOR THEIR OWN SAKE OR FOR WHO THEY ARE (CUPIDITY):

By love [charity] I mean the impulse of one's mind to enjoy God on his own account and to enjoy oneself and one's neighbor on account of God; and by lust I mean the impulse of one's mind to enjoy oneself and one's neighbor, and any corporeal thing not on account of God.

ON CHRISTIAN TEACHING, 3 X 16

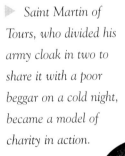

Saint Martin of Tours, who divided his army cloak in two to share it with a poor beggar on a cold night, became a model of charity in action.

The importance of Thomas Aquinas's teachings on charity are acknowledged in this fourteenth-century fresco, which shows Aquinas seated on Charity's throne.

Charitable Acts

One of the ways in which people could demonstrate the charity that moved their soul was through benevolent acts—for example, helping individuals, as when one gave alms to beggars—but charity was more often formalized through the giving of money to the church. For the wealthy charity might express itself in the endowment of a monastery or hospital. People were not supposed to draw attention to their charitable acts, as to do so would lessen the moral worth of the acts.

The charitable giving of Christians was motivated by the desire to please God and save their own soul. In practical terms, however, in the absence of such charity, there would have been no recourse for the poor and sick, who needed food, clothing, and medicine.

ANCHORITES

An anchorite was a person who lived apart from society in a special "cell," which might be a small building, often attached to a church, or even a cave. Anchorites depended on the charity of the local community for survival. An anchorite was "dead to the world" and often had the service of the dead said over him or her before being shut away. Anchorites were allowed social interaction only with a priest or to accept food. They prayed for the community and provided an opportunity for the exercise of charity. Both anchorites and the community were thought to gain spiritual benefit—anchorites in consecrating their life to God, and the community in being allowed to support one who had sacrificed all for its sake.

SEE ALSO
- **Monasticism**
- **Roman Catholic Church**
- **Thomas Aquinas**

Charlemagne

CHARLEMAGNE (742–814), a name that means Charles the Great, was king of the Franks from 768 to 814 and emperor of a large area of western Europe from 800 to 814. Through a series of military campaigns, he conquered much of western Europe and united it in a great Christian empire. As well as bringing peace and order to the lands under his rule, he also promoted learning and culture. Throughout medieval Europe, Charlemagne was considered the model of a Christian king and emperor.

Charlemagne's Conquests

Charlemagne was the eldest son of Pépin the Short, who became king of the Franks in 751. Following Pépin's death in 768, the Frankish kingdom was divided between Charlemagne and his younger brother Carloman. Three years later, on Carloman's death, Charlemagne became sole ruler of the Franks.

Charlemagne immediately began a military campaign to expand his kingdom. In the early years of his reign, he started to subdue the warlike Saxons to the northeast. In 774 he conquered the kingdom of Lombardy to the south and took the title of king of the Lombards in 778. Charlemagne fought the Saxons for the next thirty years. In 804 they finally submitted to his rule and converted to Christianity.

Charlemagne also fought a series of battles in Spain. During one of these campaigns a group of Basque warriors ambushed and killed some Frankish knights. This episode became the subject of the *Chanson de Roland* (*Song of Roland*), an epic poem. (In the poem, the attackers are Muslim Moors, not Basques.)

In 801 Charlemagne set up the Spanish March, a strongly defended area on the southern side of the Pyrenees. The independent duchy of Bavaria was incorporated into the Frankish kingdom in 788, and in 796, after a five-year campaign, the Avar people of the Danube basin were finally subdued and accepted Christianity. This victory enabled Charlemagne to create an eastern march in present-day Hungary.

▼ *The death of Roland at the battle of Roncesvalles, depicted in a fourteenth-century manuscript. This famous episode from Charlemagne's military campaign in Spain was widely illustrated in the Middle Ages.*

Emperor of the West

By 800 Charlemagne ruled an empire stretching from central Italy in the south to Denmark in the north and from Austria west to the Atlantic Ocean. The most powerful ruler since the time of the Roman emperors, he was also a devout Christian; he converted pagan peoples to Christianity and often supported the pope against his political enemies in Italy.

On Christmas Day 800, in recognition of Charlemagne's vast power and in the hope of strengthening the church's alliance with him, Pope Leo III crowned him Carolus Augustus, emperor of the Romans.

Administration and Justice

Charlemagne established his capital at Aachen and used it as a base from which to run his empire. He divided his kingdom into districts and appointed efficient officers to administer them; at the same time, he maintained central control by sending out royal inspectors to report on local conditions. He decreed that courts should sit regularly and that judges should base their decisions only on accepted law. Under Charlemagne more-efficient farming methods were introduced, new market centers were established, and silver money was coined to stimulate and facilitate trade.

The Carolingian Renaissance

Charlemagne built a large palace at Aachen and founded an academy to which many scholars of the age, including Alcuin of York, were invited. The palace academy provided an education for clergymen and

This map shows the extent of Charlemagne's empire at the time of his death in 814.

- Frankish kingdom in 768
- Territories gained by Charlemagne

trained teachers for other academies throughout the empire. Using a new style of handwriting (later known as Carolingian minuscule) that was easier to read than previous scripts, scholars at the academies collected, copied, and illustrated ancient Roman manuscripts. Charlemagne himself learned to read Latin and some Greek, although he apparently never mastered the art of writing. The revival of learning under Charlemagne is sometimes called the Carolingian Renaissance.

As well as promoting learning, Charlemagne also supported the work of architects. He had a magnificent royal chapel built at Aachen and encouraged the building of abbeys and churches throughout his empire. The monumental style of construction developed by architects during his reign became known as the Carolingian style.

Legacy

After Charlemagne's death in 814, his empire soon fell apart. In 843 it was divided into three parts, ruled by his grandsons, but by the late ninth century the empire had ceased to exist. However, the Christian cultural revival begun by Charlemagne had a lasting effect on European civilization. His empire also inspired later attempts to create a Christian empire in Europe, in particular the Holy Roman Empire, which was founded in Germany in 962.

▲ *A gold and silver bust of Charlemagne as king of the Franks, made in Aachen around 1340.*

SEE ALSO

• **Carolingians** • **Christendom** • **Education**
• **France** • **Holy Roman Empire**
• **Merovingians**

Chaucer, Geoffrey

GEOFFREY CHAUCER (c. 1345–1400) was the most important English poet of the Middle Ages. He is most famous for his *Canterbury Tales,* which he never finished. Other important works included *Troilus and Criseyde* and a translation of Boethius's *Consolation of Philosophy.* In addition to his writing, Chaucer found time to pursue a distinguished career at court and became a knight, a justice of the peace, and a member of parliament for Kent.

Geoffrey Chaucer was born in London in the 1340s, the son of a vintner. After leaving school, Chaucer became a page in the household of Lionel, the third son of

▼ *This early-fifteenth-century picture of Chaucer is from a copy of* The Canterbury Tales. *Chaucer included himself as one of the pilgrims and even told his own stories—the "Tale of Sir Thopas" and the "Tale of Melibee."*

Edward III. In 1359 Chaucer accompanied Prince Lionel to France to fight in one of the campaigns of the Hundred Years War. Chaucer was captured but ransomed by the king. He took part in the peace negotiations of 1360, the first of many royal appointments. He married Philippa, one of the queen's ladies-in-waiting, in 1366.

During his career Chaucer was on the payroll of Kings Edward III, Richard II, and Henry IV. He traveled to France, Flanders, Spain, and Italy. The duties of the offices he held included controlling customs in London and being a clerk of works at various royal estates. In the 1380s Chaucer was knighted and entered parliament. He fell on hard times after his retirement, but his fortunes revived before his death in 1400. He was buried in Poet's Corner, Westminster Abbey.

Chaucer's Writings

Chaucer may have become interested in poetry while fighting in France; soon after, he began to translate *Le roman de la rose,* a poem about courtly love. His first major work, *The Book of the Duchess* (c. 1370), was an elegy for Blanche, duchess of Lancaster. It described a dream about a knight mourning his dead love and lamenting the cruelty of Fortune. Influenced by the philosopher Boethius, Chaucer saw

Chaucer had a huge influence on the poets who came after him. John Lydgate (c. 1370–1450), for example, drew heavily on The Canterbury Tales for his own prologue to The Siege of Thebes. Lydgate is shown here leading the pilgrims in an edition of The Canterbury Tales dating from between 1455 and 1462.

Fortune as a turning wheel that created a never-ending cycle of joy and misery.

This image appeared in *Troilus and Criseyde* (c. 1382–1387), Chaucer's longest complete poem. The poem's subject—a pair of doomed lovers during the Trojan War—came from Boccaccio's *Il filostrato*.

Boccaccio's *Decameron* inspired Chaucer's last work, *The Canterbury Tales*, in which a group of pilgrims tell stories on their way to Thomas Becket's shrine. Even in its unfinished state the work displays a masterful array of plots and styles.

Chaucer was highly respected by his contemporaries. By writing in English rather than the French fashionable at court, he altered the course of English literature and even influenced the development of the language itself. His work was an inspiration to many later writers, from Shakespeare right up to the present day.

BOETHIUS 480–524

Educated at Athens and Alexandria, Boethius became consul of Rome around the age of thirty. Later, however, he was accused of treason and sentenced to death. While in prison Boethius wrote his great work, *Consolatio philosophiae (The Consolation of Philosophy)*, in which he expressed how love of God and dedication to the pursuit of knowledge were the true paths to happiness. This work, based on ancient Greek ideas, had an enormous impact on medieval thought and learning. Alfred the Great translated *Consolatio* into Anglo-Saxon, and Chaucer translated it into Middle English.

SEE ALSO

• Becket, Thomas • Boccaccio, Giovanni
• Captivity and Ransom • Hundred Years War
• Knights • Language • Literature • London
• Pilgrimage • Poetry

Childbirth and Midwifery

FOR RICH AND POOR ALIKE in the Middle Ages, childbirth, wherever in the world it took place, put the life of both mother and baby in considerable jeopardy. Children were born at home in circumstances that seldom allowed for medical intervention when, as often happened, life-threatening complications arose. The presence of a skilled, experienced midwife frequently spelled the difference between life and death for mother, child, or both.

Many women died during pregnancy and labour from hemorrhage (uncontrollable blood loss) or bacterial infection. Some women suffered horribly and sustained permanent damage when, for example, the baby was born feet first or became stuck in the birth canal. Despite some knowledge, in parts of Europe, Asia, and Africa, of herbs with painkilling properties, there was no effective way of relieving pain. The percentage of women who died in or soon after childbirth was many times higher than it presently is. In some regions, infant mortality (stillbirth or death within the first year of life) was as high as 60 percent of all births.

Childbirth and Society

The considerable dangers of pregancy and labor were exacerbated in situations of poverty, where malnutrition and squalor put an even greater strain on the health and well-being of a pregnant woman.

A poor woman usually had to work until her baby was born and returned to work soon afterward. Many women miscarried as a result of working too strenuously during pregnancy, though there is evidence of pregnant women in the later Middle Ages being advised to avoid heavy work.

Women of high status, on the other hand, withdrew to a specially prepared

chamber or suite of rooms about six weeks before giving birth and, if circumstances allowed, remained sequestered (isolated) for a further month after delivery.

Wealthier women tended to marry young, and many used a wet nurse to breast-feed their babies. Since a woman who was not breast-feeding could become pregnant again more quickly, rich women as a rule gave birth more often than poorer women (who tended to delay marrying and who breast-fed their own babies).

Childbirth and Religion

The general view of childbirth in medieval Europe was informed by Christian beliefs and practices. The pain that accompanied childbirth was thought of as God's punishment for the sin committed by Eve (as told in the book of Genesis). Women about to give birth were advised to confess and receive communion in readiness for death.

In the early Middle Ages pregnant women were deemed unclean. A woman who died in childbirth was not buried inside a church. Afer emerging from sequestration, a woman would be churched, or ritually cleansed (a practice that, by the later Middle Ages, at least, was not mandatory.)

The fear women felt may be gauged from the popularity of the birth girdle, a talisman often passed from mother to daughter that was inscribed with prayers and was thought to ensure an uncomplicated labor. Some monastic communities held birth girdles and made them available on loan.

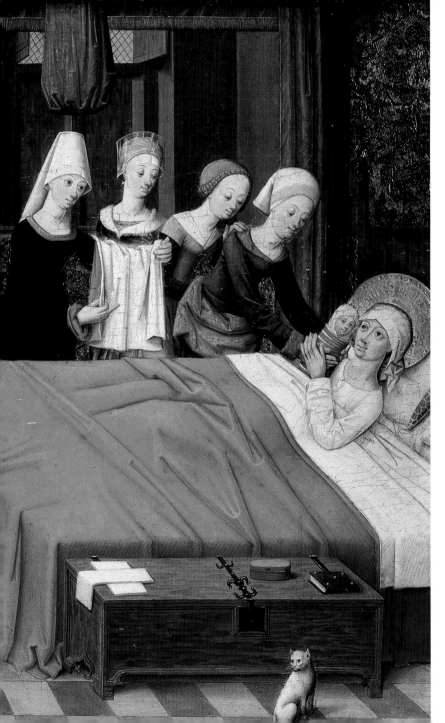

◄ *Childbirth in a rich medieval household. A midwife (right) holds a swaddled newborn child; nursemaids pour warm water (left) and hold a warmed towel (right) to bathe the child. Another maid (center) carries a soothing, nourishing drink for the mother.*

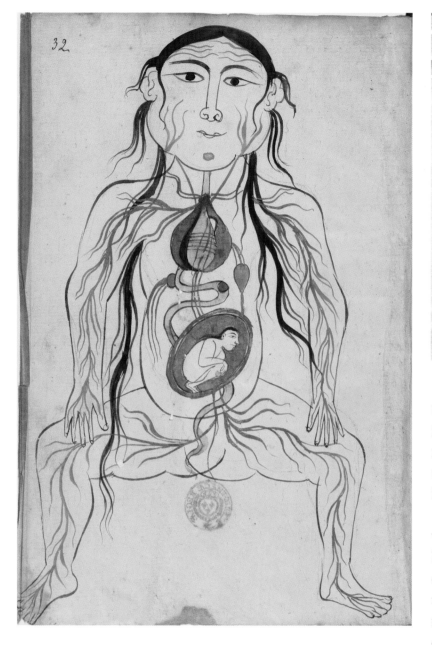

▲ *This fifteenth-century Persian anatomical diagram, typical of its period, describes the venous and arterial system of a pregnant woman.*

CHILDBIRTH IN CHINA

The practice of giving birth lying down was by no means universal. Between 1253 and 1255 William of Rubrouck, a French Franciscan friar and contemporary of Marco Polo, traveled to East Asia as an envoy of King Louis IX of France. In his narrative of the journey, which took him to the court of Mangu Khan (the king of the Mongols), he described the great ladies as "exceedingly fat" and observed that "they never lie down in bed when having their children."

Midwives often testified in legal cases relating to death during childbirth or in disputes over whether a woman had been pregnant. Midwives were vulnerable to accusations of murder, sorcery or collusion in such crimes as the substitution of babies.

Evidence that the profession of midwifery grew and developed during the Middle Ages can be found in the emerging distinction between trained and untrained midwives, in records that list midwives by name, and in the increase in treatises on obstetrics (the branch of medicine concerned with childbirth).

That medieval midwifery involved a number of superstitious practices was widely known, and in the later Middle Ages, religious reformers who sought to banish superstition from religion destroyed childbirth relics and ordered midwives not to advise their charges to use birth girdles and other such talismans.

SEE ALSO
- **Children** • **Medicine and Healing**
- **Women**

Midwives

A midwife's principal role at a birth was to reassure, to pray, and to act as a witness. A midwife also had certain medical duties. She severed the umbilical cord, washed the newborn, and sheltered it from strong light and loud noise. She was also expected to help position the baby. *The Sickness of Women,* a medical textbook, advised the midwife to rub her hands with cold thyme, lily oil, or oil of musk before doing so. A midwife also had the authority to baptize the child if its life appeared to be in danger.

Glossary

bloodletting The practice of opening a patient's vein to allow some blood to flow out.

bourse A place where commodities are bought and sold or stock is traded.

chamberlain A treasurer or financial officer of a king or a lord.

chancellor In medieval England, the king's chief minister, responsible for the smooth running of all matters of state.

elegy A poem or song of mourning, often for one who has died.

excommunicate To exclude someone from full participation in his or her church.

falconer Someone who trains falcons and other hawks used for hunting.

feng shui Chinese geomancy, a form of magic that places objects and buildings in locations that will stimulate health, wealth, and happiness.

flail A weapon whose handle is fitted with a hinged bar, often covered in iron studs or spikes.

hawking A sport in which hawks or similar birds are used to catch small prey, such as sparrows.

heretic Someone who holds religious beliefs that are contrary to the accepted doctrines of his or her faith.

humanism A belief in the overriding worth of human beings and their interests and values. Humanists typically consider secular matters more important than religious or supernatural ones.

interdict In the Roman Catholic Church, a decree depriving a person or even a whole country of access to the sacraments and to Christian burial.

mace A staff with a heavy metal head that was used as a club by both cavalry and infantry.

machicolation A hole in the base of a battlement through which missiles can be thrown.

mangonel A large wooden machine of war used to hurl rocks.

musket Originally, a small piece of artillery that fired shot of up to 10 pounds (4.5 kg). Later, a heavy shoulder-borne firearm.

ottava rima An originally Italian eight-line verse form, each line having eleven syllables, that rhymes *abababcc*.

Protestantism The branch of Christianity that issued from the Reformation. In general, Protestants deny the authority of the pope, use a simplified religious ritual conducted in a local language, and consider the Bible the sole source of revealed truth.

Reformation The early sixteenth-century religious movement, originating with Martin Luther, that broke away from the Roman Catholic Church on moral and doctrinal grounds. Its religious result was Protestantism.

Romanesque A style of architecture common in the eleventh and twelfth centuries that borrowed some features from early Christian Roman architecture and also contained elements of Byzantine and northern European styles.

sutra A sacred text of Hinduism or Buddhism containing teachings or guidelines for the faithful.

thane In Anglo-Saxon England, a kind of vassal to a feudal lord; in medieval Scotland, a feudal lord.

trebuchet A large wooden catapult (larger than a mangonel) used to hurl rocks.

vassal A person who is sworn to the service of a feudal lord and in return receives the lord's protection in times of danger.

vernacular The language of a particular people, country, or region rather than a literary or classical language, such as Latin or Greek.

Index

Page numbers in **boldface** type refer to main articles.
Page numbers in *italic* type refer to illustrations.